scrap quilt SENSATION

KATHARINE GUERRIER

D&C
David and Charles

This book is dedicated to the countless number of students who have attended my talks and classes in quilting shops, village and church halls over the U.K. for the last twenty years, many of whom have become firm friends.

A DAVID & CHARLES BOOK
Copyright © David & Charles Limited 2007

David & Charles is an F+W Publications Inc. company
4700 East Galbraith Road
Cincinnati, OH 45236

First published in the UK in 2007

Reprinted 2007 (twice)

Text and designs copyright © Katharine Guerrier 2007

Katharine Guerrier has asserted her right to be identified as author of this work in accordance with the Copyright, Designs and Patents Act, 1988.

A catalogue record for this book is available from the British Library.

ISBN-13: 978-0-7153-2451-6 hardback
ISBN-10: 0-7153-2451-9 hardback

ISBN-13: 978-0-7153-2452-3 paperback (USA only)
ISBN-10: 0-7153-2452-7 paperback (USA only)

Printed in China by SNP Leefung
for David & Charles
Brunel House   Newton Abbot   Devon

Commissioning Editor   Vivienne Wells
Editors Ame Verso and Jennifer Fox-Proverbs
Project Editor   Betsy Hosegood
Head of Design   Prudence Rogers
Designer Eleanor Stafford
Production Controller   Ros Napper

Visit our website at www.davidandcharles.co.uk

David & Charles books are available from all good bookshops; alternatively you can contact our Orderline on 0870 9908222 or write to us at FREEPOST EX2 110, D&C Direct, Newton Abbot, TQ12 4ZZ (no stamp required UK only); US customers call 800-289-0963 and Canadian customers call 800-840-5220.

Contents

Introduction

For over 20 years I have been making quilts, a natural progression from garment-making skills learned initially from my mother. As a child I remember noting that as each garment was finished, the remaining scrap fabrics were carefully hoarded away in a little bundle, against the time when the dress, shirt or whatever needed patching or mending. This never seemed to happen but the box of scraps got bigger, and even when the garments had been outworn and discarded the bundles of fabric remained. Thrift was a habit practised by my parents and instilled in me (I was born just after World War II) so waste was not an option.

This is probably the explanation for my love of scrap quilts; the idea of creating something useful and decorative from bits of material too small for any other practical purpose. My first attempts at patchwork consisted of recycling scraps from earlier dressmaking projects. The result was a hexagon quilt of random patches stitched together in a jumble of colours.

I was introduced to American block quilts through the book *A Perfect Patchwork Primer* by Beth Gutcheon, which showed me the full potential of these designs. With the help of this book I worked my way through a number of traditional blocks, learning by the 'blunder' method.

By now I was aware that other people were also making quilts. I joined the Quilter's Guild, formed in 1979, and tapped into the growing network of quilters. From these early beginnings I became totally immersed in the colours, patterns and techniques that have involved me ever since. All the original scrap fabrics have long been used up and I now buy fabric as enthusiastically as every other quilt maker, but I still adhere to the spirit of the early scrap quilts, which seem to have an enduring appeal.

Traditional pieced quilts continue to be a major inspiration for me, and some of the projects copy traditional designs with no pattern modification – Four Patch Squares (page 12), Jacob's Ladder (page 16) and Snail Trail (page 94). Individuality is added to these quilts through the choice of colour and fabric. Other projects take a traditional design and give it a twist. Take Triangle Dynamics, for example (page 28) where I have taken half-square triangle units and arranged them in a number of different blocks to create an array of diamonds, zigzags, stars and pinwheels in a single quilt. In Cropped Pinwheels (page 78) I cut the pinwheels and set them into light or dark triangles that were then arranged Log Cabin style to create a secondary design, using my modern, modified block in a traditional way.

Further variations on traditional themes are provided in the other quilts. In Dark Stars (page 46), for example, there are three traditional star blocks, but these are in two sizes and with many variations, creating a mosaic-like effect. Likewise, I took the traditional idea of a sampler but set my blocks at angles and added saw-tooth sashing to give my Sampler Quilt (page 62) added excitement and a real sense of movement.

Miniature Barn Raising quilt. Traditional blocks, such as Log Cabin, continue to be a major inspiration

Colour choices

Quilters are often anxious about colour, and I am frequently asked if I have any kind of formula for choosing and combining colours and fabrics. My choices seem to be mostly intuitive but I have tried to explain how I arrive at them in Fabulous Fabrics (page 6). The fabric notes accompanying each quilt also offer tips on colour and fabric choices. If I were asked to give one piece of advice with regard to colour I would just say 'audition' sets of fabrics and attempt to create collections that harmonize well together. More fabrics can be added in as you work on your quilt. Decisions can be hard to make. I have been known to unpick and replace a block from a finished quilt top because I was unhappy with the result. If you have room for a design wall (a vertical surface onto which you can fix up work in progress), this is a great help. Standing away from your work helps to pinpoint areas that need adjustment.

I hope you will enjoy creating your own scrap quilts from my patterns as much as I have enjoyed making the originals.

About this book...

This book builds up from very simple scrap quilts at the beginning that are suitable for a novice, such as Four-Patch Squares on page 12, to more advanced or experimental pieces like Cropped Pinwheels (page 78) and the Triptych Wall Hanging on page 100. All the pieces can be rotary cut, and quick-piecing methods are used to speed up the construction, but if you prefer to work with templates these can be cut from paper using the measurements given with each pattern.

Fabulous Fabrics

If I compare my most recent quilt with an earlier one, Light Maze, shown right, which I made in 1983, the most striking difference is the much wider range of fabrics I now use. I can still remember searching for the fabrics to make Light Maze: there were not many quilt shops then – if you went to a regular dress fabric shop you were lucky to get more than three shades of one colour, and most of the patterned fabrics were small flower prints.

Today, patchworkers must have the widest and most exciting range of fabrics available ever. Fabric designers and manufacturers are constantly bringing out new patterns and collections so it becomes increasingly difficult to make decisions when you are in the quilt shops. We can get round this to some extent by buying themed or co-ordinating packs, but once these are unpacked and ready to use we still have to decide what goes where in the quilt blocks. If you are a newcomer to quilt making, it may seem strange to buy pieces of fabric with no particular project in mind but the contemporary scrap quilt needs a stash – a collection of fabrics to draw on rather like an artist's palette of paints. This is the contemporary equivalent of the scrap bag of earlier days, with its carefully hoarded bits of fabric ready to be made into quilts.

Light Maze, one of my earlier quilts

A selection of fabrics with light values – I avoid white, preferring fabrics with pastel backgrounds

Fabrics with mid values. Sort out your lights and darks first; those that fall into neither category are your mid-value fabrics

Fabrics with dark values add richness and depth

Finding fabrics

Fabrics left over from other projects are a good starting point and you could build on this collection to increase the available options. Try to include dark, medium and light fabrics. Mix the patterns: floral, geometric, striped, directional prints, abstract, finely detailed and larger scale prints. I don't use any plain fabric in my scrap quilts but this does not mean they cannot be included. I tend only to buy small pieces – quarters or half metres – and collect them whenever I visit a quilt shop. If friends offer bits of fabric they are discarding, my rule is 'never say no!' You never know what vintage treasures may come to light. More than once I have looked at a particular piece of fabric and thought 'I'll never find a use for that' but usually these bits find their way into one of my quilts, so I rarely throw anything out.

Bright fabrics add 'sparkle' and provide focal points

When selecting fabrics for a scrap quilt I try to use colours and patterns that harmonize. This is my personal choice and not necessarily the only one, and when I teach classes my students sometimes make what seem to me to be surprising choices that also work well. Students or teachers, we can all learn from each other.

Most of the light fabrics I use don't contain white backgrounds; I rely on a more muted appearance created by pastel coloured backgrounds or greys and beige. I look for tone-on-tone fabrics where there is not a high contrast within the fabric.

The sort of fabric I would avoid would be the strong black and white striped or checked fabric or a dark print on a light ground. These are difficult to classify as dark, medium or light and may be too eye catching, distracting from the overall design.

Usually, I mix all the colours together in a quilt (see Splashes of Colour, page 56). If you find this too much of a challenge, try limiting your colour palette, as in Dark Stars (page 46) and Snail Trail (page 94), both of which use mainly blue fabrics.

Bright fabrics such as yellow, orange and lime green can add 'sparkle' to a quilt, creating focus points and keeping up the interest for the viewer (and the maker). These bright colours need to be balanced over the quilt surface to keep the eye moving. This is where a design wall or a large pinboard is a useful tool – as you work, put up the blocks and stand a distance away from them. Move them around, change the composition, make decisions about how to progress and tailor blocks to those you have already made.

I avoid fabrics that contain strong contrasts, like these, because they are difficult to define and can be too eye-catching, distracting attention from the overall design

These three blocks show how your use of different values affects the final look of the block

Value variations

Many of my quilt patterns rely on contrast: critically placed values in light, medium and dark fabrics. Typical traditional examples of these are the Log Cabin and the Snail Trail blocks. This leads on to the question many students in my classes ask: 'Is this a light or a dark fabric?' The answer depends on what you put next to it. A medium fabric can often act as a light or a dark, as illustrated by the sample blocks above. There are other ways to provide contrast. Try varying the scale of the prints, or teaming a large-scale pattern with a plain fabric in similar values. You will probably learn most from your own experiments. Make sample blocks, look at other people's quilts and analyse why you think they are successful. Be adventurous with your colour selections, building confidence to try out ever-new combinations.

When one of my quilts is finished I often have a number of unused blocks, but I don't consider that I wasted time making them and they often find their way into another project, maybe into a pieced back. Quilt making is an adventure with colour, requiring only some fabrics and a few basic pieces of equipment, making it accessible to anybody with a creative spirit and a willingness to learn the basic sewing skills required. Be warned though; it can be very addictive!

Patterns or plains? With fairly plain fabrics use colour values to bring out the block design. When fabrics are patterned you can create contrast with a change of pattern scale as well as through value differences

Simple Squares

A quilt with a pattern of regular squares is a good choice for a newcomer to patchwork and it's a traditional design that has stood the test of time. Progress is fast and there are no awkward angles to piece together so you can concentrate on choosing fabrics and enjoy blending and contrasting colours and values. If you want to work with squares but would like more of a challenge take a look at Squares and Diamonds on page 14. The squares are all the same size but some are first pieced to create randomly placed diamond units.

Four-Patch Squares, 43 x 39in (109.25 x 99cm)
Quilted by Rosemary Archer of Frome Valley Quilting

Squares and Diamonds, 50 x 42½in (127 x 108cm)
Quilted by Rosemary Archer of Frome Valley Quilting

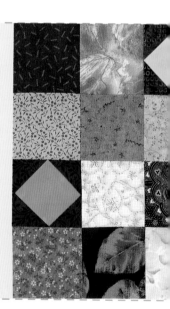

Fabric Notes...

Four-Patch Squares

The four-patch units – the smaller squares – are made with dark/light pairs. I used a number of bright yellows and oranges as well as other light fabrics teamed with the dark ones to give the quilt added warmth. For the larger squares I selected medium values in a number of different colours.

Squares and Diamonds

Go with colour combinations and arrangements that you find pleasing and don't think too hard while contrasting, blending and matching colours. View the quilt top from a distance to check that all the eye-catching colours and fabrics are well balanced as you work.

Four-Patch Squares

Finished block
4 x 4in (10 x 10cm)

Finished quilt
43 x 39in (109.25 x 99cm)

Fabric requirements
Cotton fabric: a total of 2¼ yards (2 metres) of fabric scraps in a mix of colours and patterns. Cut the larger squares to 4½in (11.5cm) and the smaller ones to 2½in (6.25cm)
Backing: cotton fabric(s) made up to 48 x 44in (122 x 112cm)
Binding: ½ yard (0.5metre)
Wadding: piece 48 x 44in (122 x 112cm)

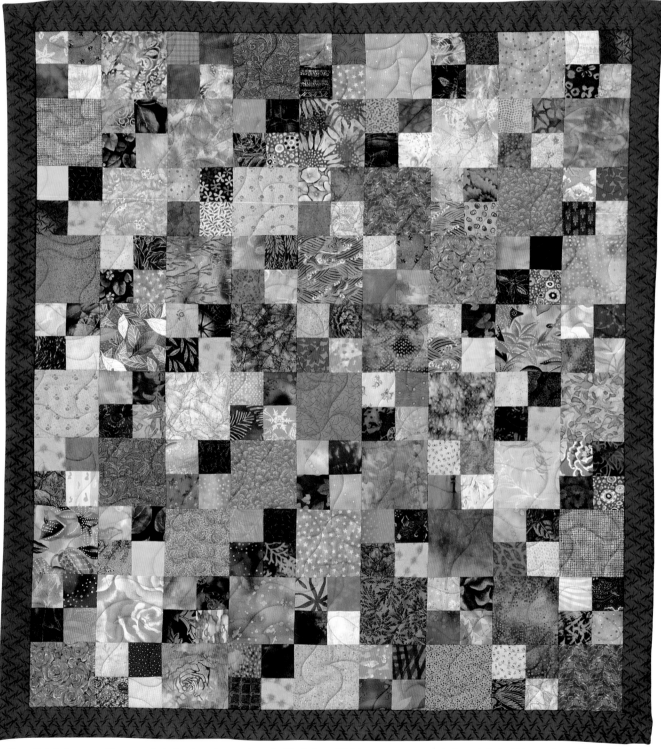

Four-Patch Squares. The overall design is a chequerboard with dark and light squares arranged alternately, but I have strayed from this rule

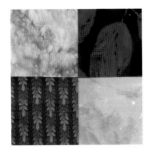

Fig 1. Four-patch unit

Cutting the squares

Cut the squares for the four-patch blocks to 2½in (6.25cm). Altogether you will need 180; start with 25–30 and then add to them as you work. Select a variety of colours and tonal values; darks, lights and brights for the small squares. Cut the larger squares 4½in (11.5cm) – you will need 45 of these.

Making the four-patch units

1 Pick 2 of the smaller squares in a darkish value and 2 in a light or bright value. Stitch the squares together in contrasting pairs then stitch the pairs together to make the four-patch units, as shown in Fig 1.

2 Make 45 four-patch units.

Joining the units

Referring to the photograph left as a guide, arrange the larger squares and four-patch blocks alternately on a design wall to create a pleasing balance of colours and values. When you are happy with the result, stitch the squares and blocks together in columns, then stitch the columns together to complete the quilt top, as shown in Fig 2.

Tip
Reducing bulk

Press seams in opposite directions as you work to minimize bulk on the final seams.

Quilting the layers

1 Cut the wadding and the backing fabric so that they are 1½in (4cm) larger all round than the quilt top. Assemble the 3 layers of the quilt with the quilt top centred on the wadding and the backing fabric underneath. Pin and then tack (baste) horizontal and vertical grid lines about 4in (10cm) apart across the entire quilt.

2 Quilt as desired by hand or machine (see page 116) using an appropriate quilting thread. Alternatively, enlist the services of a quilter with a long-arm quilting machine (see page 116).

Binding and finishing

1 Cut two binding strips 47 x 8in (120 x 20.25cm) and two 51 x 8in (130 x 20.25cm) piecing them together as necessary to make up the required lengths.

2 Trim the wadding and backing to extend to 1½in (4cm) beyond the quilt top.

3 Press the binding in half lengthways with wrong sides facing and attach it to the quilt following the instructions for broad binding with stitched mitres on page 119.

4 Don't forget to add a label to the back of the quilt stating who made it and when plus any other information desired.

Fig 2. Join the blocks into columns and then join the columns, arranging the four-patch units as shown

Squares and Diamonds

Finished block
2½ x 2½in (6.25 x 6.25cm)
Finished quilt
50 x 42½in (127 x 108cm)

Squares and Diamonds. A wide, dark-toned border draws the eye in to the colourful patchwork centre

Fig 1. 16-square block

Assembly

Although this is an all-over pattern of squares it is more convenient when making up the quilt top to assemble it in blocks or sections. I made these 4 squares across by 4 down (16 squares to a block) as in Fig 1, and 5 squares across by 4 down (20 squares to a block) to get the patchwork panel the size I wanted.

Cutting the squares

Cut the squares to 3in (7.5cm). You will need 208 squares; start with 30–50 and add to them as you work.

Making and joining the units

1 Select 16 squares and arrange them on a flat surface. Choose 2 to be converted into the diamonds. I picked the brighter colours such as yellow, orange and pink for these. To make one of the diamonds, select a contrasting fabric for the corners and cut 4 squares 1¾in (4.5cm). Follow the procedure for making a diamond in a square on page 115 to complete the diamond detail. For each block of squares make 2 diamonds.

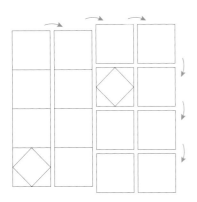

Fig 2. Assemble the squares into blocks

2 Assemble the 16 squares together in a block of 4 x 4, positioning the diamonds randomly in the set. Stitch 4 columns of squares then stitch the columns together (see Figs 1 and 2).

3 Make 8 blocks with 16 squares. Now make 4 blocks with 20 squares, each 5 squares across and 4 down.

4 Arrange the blocks to distribute the colours and the diamonds to create a pleasing balance and stitch them together (see Fig 3).

Adding the border

Cutting across the width of the border fabric from selvedge to selvedge, cut 4 strips 5½in (14cm). Stitch 2 border strips to opposite sides along the length of the panel, trim them to match then press the seams. Attach the remaining 2 strips to the top and bottom; trim to fit.

Quilting and finishing

Assemble the quilt top, wadding and backing and complete the quilt as explained on pages 116–118.

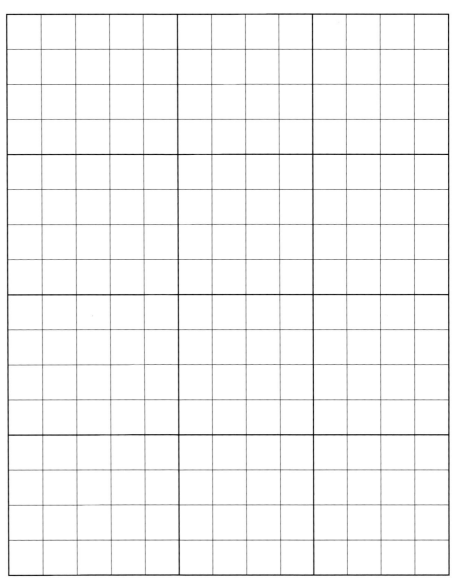

Fig 3. Block arrangement

Jacob's Ladder

This traditional design is built out of two basic blocks – the four-patch unit introduced on page 12 and half-square triangle units that can be made using quick-piecing techniques. It is straightforward to construct and makes good use of small fabric scraps.

Making this quilt teaches you how to position dark and light values within your blocks, creating the necessary contrast to build up the distinctive overall diagonal pattern. When the values have been placed correctly and the blocks joined together a new, larger pattern forms and it becomes difficult to identify the individual blocks. You can make this quilt as large as you like.

Jacob's Ladder, 64 x 64in (162.5 x 162.5cm)
Quilted by Beryl Cadman of Custom Quilting

Fabric Notes...

When I am working on a quilt with many different fabrics I often make a few blocks without thinking too hard about which fabrics to select from the scrap bag. Once I have a few blocks I put them on the design wall, stand back and consider how to proceed. Subsequent blocks are then tailored to what I have made. In this case red seemed to be dominant so I continued to use red fabrics, especially for the triangles. My smallest pieces of fabric are jumbled together in a large box and this was raided for the smaller squares, giving a fairly random choice of whatever was big enough.

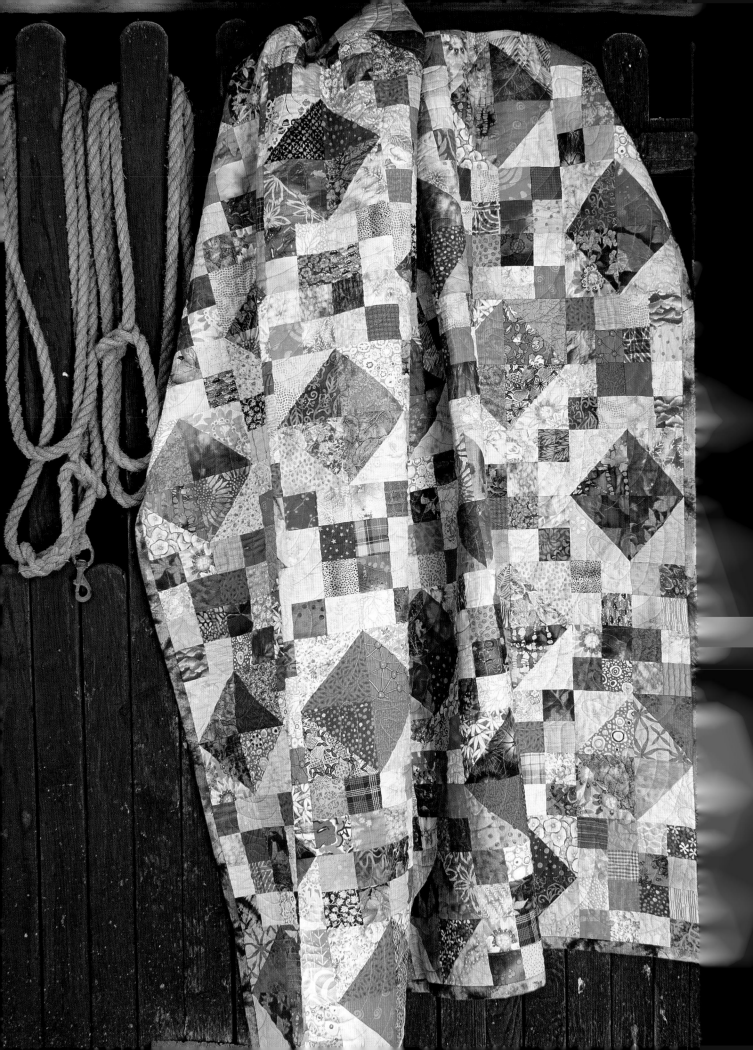

Jacob's Ladder. A close contrast between the dark and light values and use of warm red and orange fabrics add to the richness of this quilt

Jacob's Ladder

Jacob's Ladder

Finished block
8 x 8in (20.25 x 20.25cm)
Finished quilt
64 x 64in (162.5 x 162.5cm)

Fabric requirements

Cotton fabric: a total of 5½ yards (5 metres) of fabric scraps in light and dark patterned fabrics
Backing: cotton fabric(s) made up to 72 x 72in (183 x 183cm)
Binding: 1 yard (0.75 metre) of cotton fabric
Wadding: 72 x 72in (183 x 183cm)

Assembly

Each block is composed of 2 triangle units and 2 four-patch units. You will need 49 blocks for the centre panel and 28 half blocks to create an integral border.

1 dark square and make half-square triangle units (Fig 1) as explained on page 113. For the entire quilt you will need 128 units.

Making the four-patch units

Cut 2½in (6.25cm) squares from dark and light values. Cut 20–30 to begin with. Stitch 1 light and 1 dark square together; repeat to make a second pair. Press the seams open then join the pairs to produce a four-patch unit as shown in Fig 2. You will need 128 of these units.

Fig 1. Half-square triangle unit

Making the triangle units

For the triangle units cut squares 4⅞in (12.5cm) in light and dark fabrics. Start by cutting 5–10 of each value. Place these right sides together in pairs of 1 light and

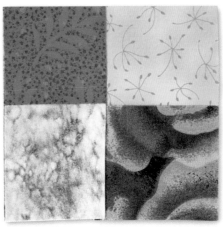

Fig 2. Four-patch unit

Tip
Extra blocks
Don't worry about making too many blocks – any leftover once the quilt is pieced together can be put to good use in your next quilt!

Quilt detail. The finished block comprises 2 half-square triangle units and 2 four-patch units. When stitched together, these blocks are 'lost' in the larger, overall design. The quilt stitching, here simple curving lines, should further unite the quilt

Joining the units

1 Lay out 2 triangle units and 2 four-patch units in the correct order and stitch together, first into pairs, as indicated by the red arrows in Fig 3, and then into 1 larger unit to complete the block.

2 Your finished block should look like the one in Fig 4. Make 49 blocks.

3 Referring to Fig 5, opposite, as a guide, and using a design wall if possible, arrange your blocks to create the centre panel. There should be 7 blocks in each row and 7 rows in total.

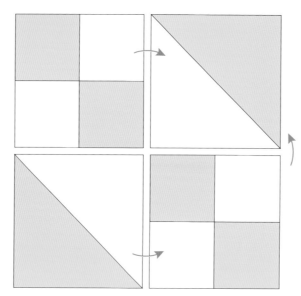

*Fig 3. Assemble the triangle units
and four-patch units into blocks*

Fig 4. The finished block. Note the placement of light and dark tones

Adding the border

1 Make 30 triangle units and 30 four-patch units as explained before.

2 Arrange the units around the quilt so that the dark triangles form diamonds with those in the edges of the quilt, and the four-patch units extend the panels of squares into the border.

3 Stitch the border units together in strips. Join these to the top and bottom of the quilt and then to the sides, as illustrated in Fig 5, below.

Quilting the layers

1 Cut the wadding and the backing fabric so that they are 1½in (4cm) larger all round than the quilt top. Assemble the 3 layers of the quilt with the quilt top centred on the wadding and the backing fabric underneath. Pin and then tack (baste) horizontal and vertical grid lines about 4in (10cm) apart across the entire quilt.

2 Quilt as desired by hand or machine (see page 116) using an appropriate quilting thread. Alternatively, enlist the services of a quilter with a long-arm quilting machine (see page 116).

Binding and finishing

1 Cut binding strips 2½in (6.25cm) wide, piecing them together as necessary to make up the required length.

2 Trim the wadding and backing fabrics a scant ¼in (0.75cm) beyond the edge of the quilt top.

3 Press the binding in half lengthways with wrong sides facing and attach it to the quilt following the instructions for straight binding with square corners on page 118.

4 Don't forget to add a label to the back of the quilt stating who made it and when plus any other information desired.

Fig 5. Border placement

Strictly Triangles

If you think that quilts based on triangles are too difficult for you then you can think again because this quilt is deceptively simple and is actually built up in square blocks. Inspired by a 19th-century charm quilt of triangles, this variation is an explosion of colour and a feast for the eyes, and can be made any size from lap quilt to kingsize.

In a charm quilt each fabric is used only once but my fabric collection is not so extensive that I could do this, so there are repeats. I also added in the detail of the smaller triangles, grouped into blocks of four identical units, to make an all-over pattern of triangles in two sizes. The small units are made in exactly the same way as the larger triangle units so the technique is very simple.

Strictly Triangles, 90 x 96in (229 x 244cm)
Quilted by Beryl Cadman of Custom Quilting

Fabric Notes...

I used patterned fabrics for this quilt but you can use some plain ones too, if desired. The large triangle blocks are made in dark/medium values while the smaller ones are in bright fabrics teamed with darks to make focal points across the quilt. If you want to achieve a similar effect of variety, you can increase your fabric collection by buying 4in (10cm) widths of fabric across the bolt. This will yield 10 squares 4in (10cm) to make the larger triangles. This way you can get 10 different fabrics for the price of 4 fat quarters. Choose a good mix of colours, patterns and scales of prints, including geometrics, florals, stripes, checks and textured patterns, marbled and hand-dyed fabrics.

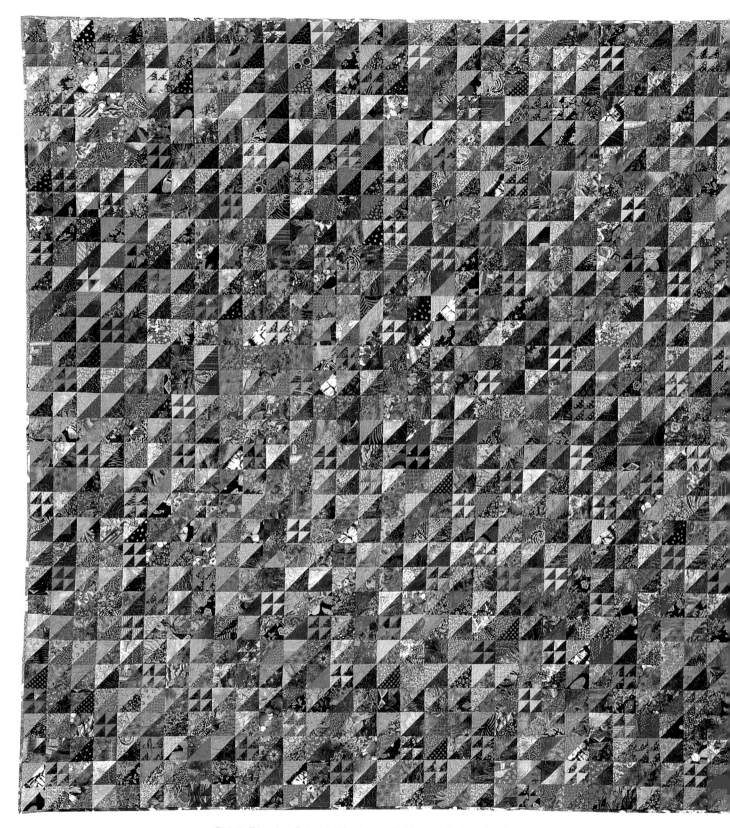

Strictly Triangles. Select bright colours for the smaller triangles to create a jewel-like effect on the surface of the quilt

Strictly Triangles

Finished block
12 x 12in (30.5 x 30.5cm)
Finished quilt
90 x 96in (229 x 244cm)

Fabric requirements

Cotton fabric: a total of 12 yards (11 metres) of fabric scraps
Binding: 1 yard (1 metre) of cotton fabric
Backing: cotton fabric(s) made up to 98 x 104in (249 x 264.25cm)
Wadding: 98 x 104in (249 x 264.25cm)

Cutting the fabrics

1 Sort your fabrics into values. The larger triangles are mainly cut from dark/medium selections and the smaller ones from bright/dark tones.

2 From the dark and medium selections cut 40 squares 4in (10.25cm) of each to begin with. You can add more to these as you work.

Making and joining the units

You will need a total of 960 units – about 840 half-square triangle units and 120 of the small-triangle units. As these are made in square blocks this is quicker and easier than you might think.

1 Place the squares right sides together in pairs and make half-square triangle units as explained on page 113. Trim the resulting bi-coloured squares to exactly 3½in (9cm), making sure that the seam-line still runs from corner to corner (Fig 1).

2 To make the other triangle units cut 2 pairs of bright/dark squares 2⅜in (6cm) and repeat the procedure for half-square triangles to make 4 bi-coloured squares. Stitch these together to make each small-triangle unit, as shown in Fig 2. This will also measure 3½in (9cm).

3 Although this is an all-over design, the triangle units are stitched together in blocks for ease of handling. When you have prepared an adequate number of large and small triangle units, lay them on a flat surface in sets of 16. Most of the blocks in this quilt have 14 of the larger triangle units and 2 of the smaller ones. Just a few have 3 of the smaller ones. Position the smaller ones randomly as you construct the blocks. As you stitch the units together be sure to place all the dark fabrics on the same side of the diagonal divisions, as shown in Fig 3.

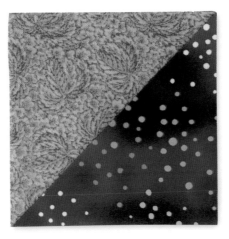

Fig 1. Half-square triangle unit

Fig 2. Small-triangle unit

Fig 3. Block of 16 units with the dark triangles all on the bottom right

4 Cut more squares and repeat the procedure to make about 840 of the large triangle units and 120 of the smaller ones. Continue to lay them out and stitch them in blocks as before. Some of the blocks have extra units to make up the size – make 40 blocks of 16 units (4 x 4) and 16 blocks of 20 units (5 x 4).

5 When you have completed the blocks, stitch them together using the photograph on page 24 and Fig 4 below as your guides. Remember to maintain the same positioning of the darker blocks at all times. Notice from the plan below that all the larger blocks (those containing 20 units) are placed in two columns on the left. To

avoid stitching long seams, which can result in distortion, join the blocks in groups of say, 4 x 4 or 4 x 3 units, then join the groups together to complete the quilt top.

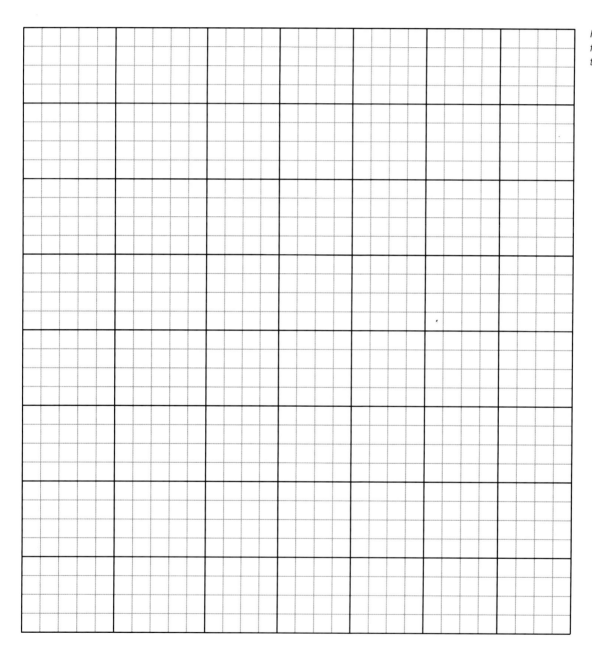

Fig 4. Layout plan for placement of the blocks

Quilting the layers

1 Cut the wadding and the backing fabric so that they are 1½in (4cm) larger all round than the quilt top. Assemble the 3 layers of the quilt with the quilt top centred on the wadding and the backing fabric underneath. Pin and then tack (baste) horizontal and vertical grid lines about 4in (10cm) apart across the entire quilt.

2 Quilt as desired by hand or machine (see page 116) using an appropriate quilting thread. Alternatively, enlist the services of a quilter with a long-arm quilting machine (see page 116).

Quilt detail. This quilt was machine stitched in curving lines for a fluid look. The stitching lines are placed quite close together, increasing the luscious, padded look of the quilt

Binding and finishing

1 Cut binding strips 2½in (6.25cm) wide, piecing them together as necessary to make up the required length.

2 Fold the binding strips in half lengthways, wrong sides together and press. Place the raw edges of the binding against the outer edges of the quilt top and stitch, taking a ¼in (7mm) seam allowance and starting and finishing the stitching line ¼in (7mm) from the side edge. Trim the wadding and backing fabrics to size.

3 Using a stitched mitre at the corners (see page 119) bind the edges of the quilt and hand stitch to the back.

4 Don't forget to add a label to the back of the quilt stating who made it and when plus any other information desired.

Tip

Lighter weight

The number of seams in this quilt top makes it quite heavy so choose a thin wadding and a light fabric for the backing.

Triangle Dynamics

With its rich visual texture and seemingly complex design, this showstopper is actually deceptively simple to construct. The patterns seem to merge together into an overall design so it is difficult to identify the individual blocks, but the quilt is constructed in units, making it easier than it looks. Because the blocks can be made into different patterns and because there are additional smaller scale details, you are making decisions as you work rather than all at the beginning, so this quilt keeps your interest throughout its construction. Quilts made using this formula are open to individual interpretation, making them unique to the maker.

You can make the quilt any size divisible by the 12in (30cm) square blocks. The basic unit is a 3in (finished) square made of two half-square triangles. The smaller scale details can be fitted into the grid of the blocks, adding focus points and 'sparkle' to the quilt.

Triangle Dynamics, 51 x 51in (129.5 x 129.5cm)
Quilted by the author

Fabric Notes...

When buying fabrics there always seem to me to be more appealing dark fabrics than there are light ones. This quilt reflects my collection before I started making a determined effort to acquire a bigger range of light fabrics, as my quilts seemed to be getting increasingly darker. Without the lime green, yellow and pink in the mini blocks the darker fabrics would dominate. I have made several version of this pattern in a number of different sizes. The possible variations seem to be endless as no two turn out the same. I used patterned fabrics but you could use plains too, if desired. When making the mini blocks, choose bright colours teamed with dark or use high-contrast dark/light pairs to make the pinwheels more visible.

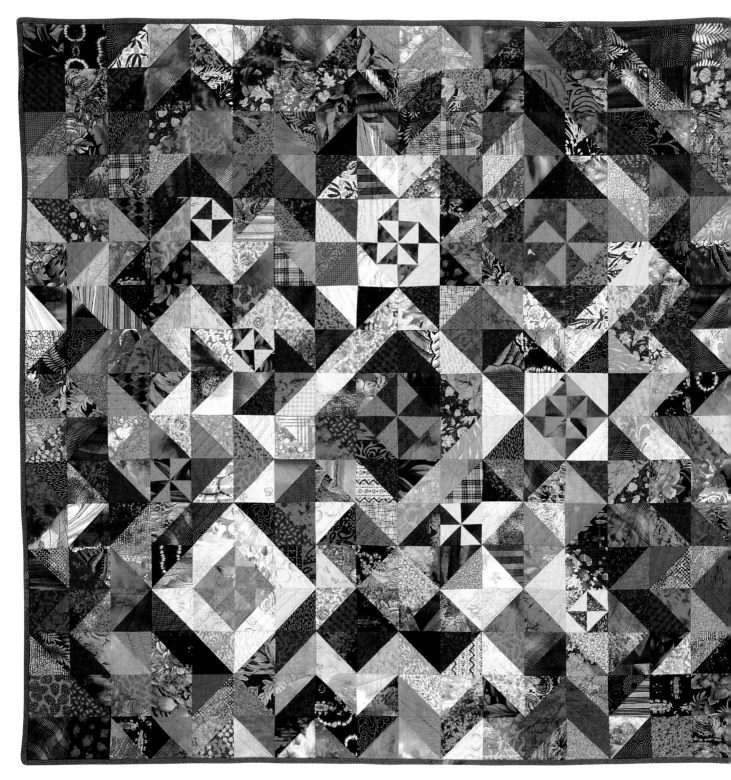

Triangle Dynamics. The nostalgic appeal of the scrap quilt is combined here with inventive ways of using half-square triangle units. It will keep your mind active and creative all the way up to completion

Triangle Dynamics

Finished block
12 x 12in (30.5 x 30.5cm)
Finished quilt
51 x 51in (129.5 x 129.5cm)

Fabric requirements

Cotton fabric: a total of 5½ yards (5 metres) of scraps for the basic units – anything larger than a 4in (10cm) square. For the mini blocks the largest square required is 4¼in (11cm)
Backing: cotton fabric(s) made up to 59 x 59in (150 x 150cm)
Binding: 1 yard (1 metre) of cotton fabric
Wadding: 59 x 59in (150 x 150cm)

Assembly

The quilt is assembled from half-square triangle units arranged in a variety of ways to create 12in (30.5cm) blocks and from mini units, also based on half-square triangles, made up to fit into the blocks. Work in the order given to make a total of 9 blocks, some including the mini units. You will need additional fabrics for the chevron border.

Making the basic block

One basic block is made up from 16 units arranged in a block of 4 x 4.

1 Half-triangle units can be arranged in blocks of 4 x 4 in a variety of ways to create many intriguing patterns. Fig 2 shows six options, which are shown made up overleaf. Refer to Fig 2 below and to the photographs on page 32

to make 1 or 2 blocks in different designs. Stars, diamonds and zigzags can all be created just by altering the orientation of the seams. You will probably discover more than are illustrated here.

2 Next make up some of the mini units as explained on pages 33–35 and make further blocks using these. Make as many different patterns as you like.

Fig 1. Bi-coloured half-square triangle unit

Making the half-square triangle units

From the light and dark fabrics cut 3⅞in (10cm) squares in at least 32 different fabrics. Place these right sides together in pairs of one light and one dark fabric. Using the technique for making half-square triangle units on page 113, make up 32 or more bi-coloured squares. Trim off all the extending points from the seam allowances.

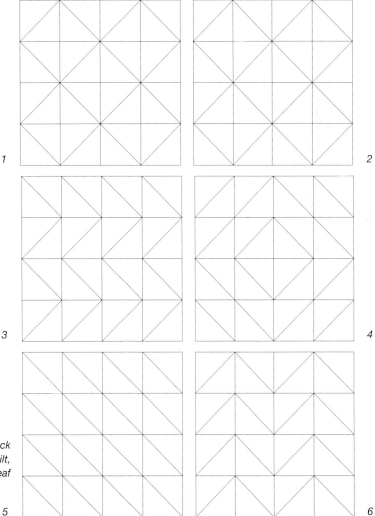

Fig 2. Potential block arrangements for your quilt, shown made up overleaf

Fig 3. This block is arranged following design 1 on page 31 to create an attractive cross formation. For this design to work, as for all the designs, it is important to place light and dark toned triangles carefully.

Fig 4. Large light and dark squares set on point are created by placing light and dark triangles together in blocks following design 2 on page 31. This simple arrangement is very striking.

Fig 5. Chevrons are created here by arranging the half-square triangle blocks more or less as shown in design 3 on page 31. You don't have to stick religiously to a design – letting it 'fall apart' can create a sense of movement.

Fig 6. Half-square triangle units are arranged in this block so 4 pale triangles join in the centre to create a small diamond with a dark frame around it. Mid-tone fabrics surround the block, making the central design stand out. This is design 4 on page 31.

Fig 7. This block follows design 5 on page 31. Note that the sharper the contrast between tones, the bolder the design will be. By utilizing some mid tones the design becomes more mysterious and intriguing.

Fig 8. Design 6 has a column of half-triangle blocks with the dark triangles positioned at bottom right followed by a column with the dark triangles positioned at top right. The resulting block looks surprisingly intricate.

Fig 9. Mini unit A creates a
central pinwheel

Making mini unit A

There are three different variations of the
mini blocks: A, B and C. The A block
will replace four of the basic units and
introduce the larger pinwheel as part of
the block.

1 Choose 3 or more fabrics: 2 for the
centre pinwheel and 1–4 for the corners
– the pinwheel fabrics should be light or
bright and dark and the corners fairly light.

2 Cut 1 square 4¼in (11cm) of each of
the pinwheel fabrics and place these right
sides together. Draw 2 diagonal lines
across the wrong side of the lighter fabric.
Stitch in a 'windmill' pattern as illustrated in
Fig 10, sewing ¼in (0.75cm) away from the
drawn lines, from the edge of the squares
to the centre.

3 Cut across both diagonals. This will yield
4 bi-coloured triangles.

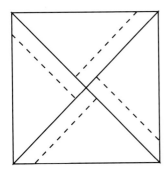

Fig 10. Stitch the two pinwheel fabrics
together in a 'windmill' pattern

4 Using the remaining fabric(s) selected for
the corners, cut 2 squares 3⅞in (11cm).
Divide these into 4 triangles by cutting
across 1 diagonal. Now stitch 1 pieced
triangle to 1 of these corner triangles.
Repeat 3 more times as shown in Fig 11.

5 Stitch the resulting squares together in
the sequence illustrated in Fig 11 to make
the A block.

Making a block with unit A

Make a block using 12 half-square triangle
units and replacing the other 4 with the A
unit. Follow the arrangement shown in Fig
12 below or use your own design.

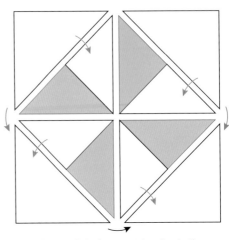

Fig 11. Join the new triangles to the
bi-coloured triangles to make the A unit

Fig 12. A 12in (30.5cm) block created using the A unit and 12 half-square triangle units

Fig 13. Mini unit B is made from four quarter-square triangle units attached to triangles

Making mini unit B

The B block is also a pinwheel but made on a smaller scale. Like mini block A, it can be used to replace 4 of the half-square triangle units.

1 Choose 2 high-contrast fabrics in light or bright and dark combinations for the pinwheel as in Fig 13.

2 Cut 2 squares $3^3/_8$in (8.5cm) from each of the fabrics.

3 Place your squares right sides together in pairs of 1 light and 1 dark fabric and repeat the 'windmill' sewing sequence as for the A block (see page 33). Cut across the diagonal lines to create the bi-coloured triangles. This time you will have 8.

4 Join these bi-coloured triangles in pairs to make 4 quarter-square triangle units, as shown in Fig 14, below.

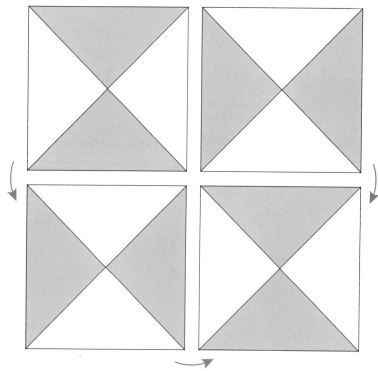

Fig 15. Join the quarter-square triangle units to make the pinwheel

5 Stitch the quarter-square triangle units together in pairs, then join the pairs as shown in Fig 15 to make the pinwheel.

6 Cut 2 squares $3^7/_8$in (11cm) for the corner triangles then cut these into triangles by cutting across 1 diagonal. These can be all the same fabric or 4 different ones to add to the scrap look. Referring to Fig 16, right, add these triangles to opposite sides of the pinwheel. Press the seams then add the other 2 and press again.

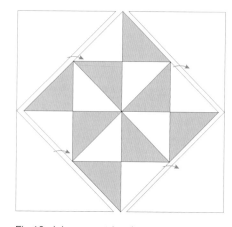

Fig 16. Join corner triangles to the pinwheel

Making a block with unit B

Make a block using 12 half-square triangle units and replacing the other 4 with the B unit. Follow the arrangement shown in Fig 17, right, or use your own design.

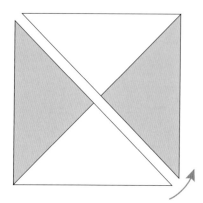

Fig 14. Join the bi-coloured triangles in pairs to make quarter-square triangle units

Fig 17. Create a 12in (30.5cm) block using the B unit and 12 half-square triangle units

Making mini unit C

This unit can replace one of the half-triangle units and can be scattered across the quilt to add jewel points. Once again, it is based on half-triangle units that can be arranged to create different effects.

1 Choose 2 high-contrast fabrics in light or bright and dark combinations for the unit like the ones shown in Fig 19.

2 Cut 2 squares 2³/₈in (6cm) from each fabric. Place these right sides together and make half-square triangle units as explained on page 113.

3 Join the resulting 4 squares to create an eye-catching block, referring to Figs 18 and 19 for possible arrangements.

Making a block with unit C

Make a block using 14 half-square triangle units and replacing the other 2 with C units. Follow the arrangement shown in the Fig 20 or use your own design.

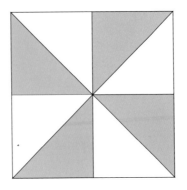
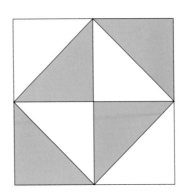
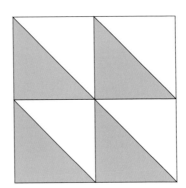
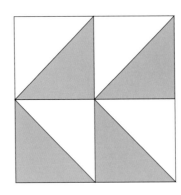

Fig 18. Four potential C units

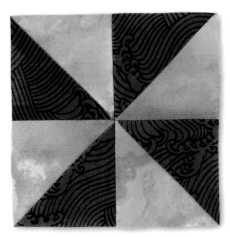
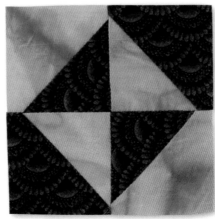

Fig 20. Create a 12in (30.5cm) block using a C unit and half-square triangle units

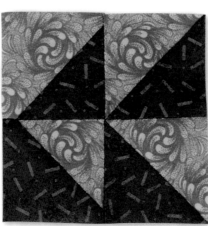

Fig 19. Here are the units shown in the diagrams in Fig 18 made up in fabrics

Joining the blocks

When you have made a number of blocks arrange them edge-to-edge, using a design wall, if possible. Move them around until you are satisfied with the overall effect. You will find that the individual blocks will 'disappear' to make an overall pattern. My quilt has 9 blocks, but you can use more or less to fulfil the size requirement of you quilt. (Note that the border will add 6in (15cm) or 9in (23cm) to each side.)

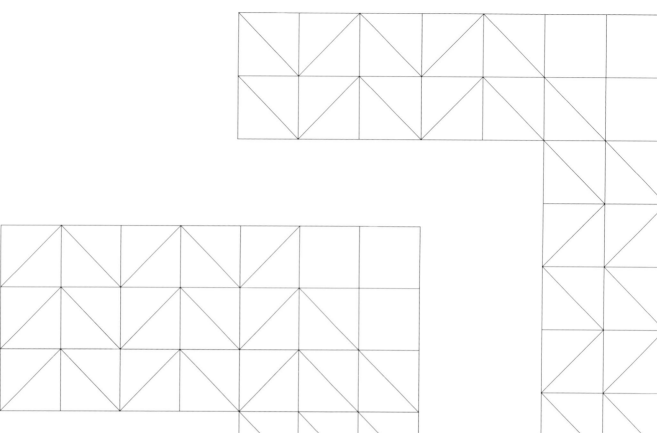

Making the chevron border

The border comprises basic half-triangle blocks arranged over 2 or 3 rows in a simple chevron pattern around the edge of the quilt.

1 Make more of the basic 3in (7.5cm) half-square triangle units. (These are 3½in (9cm) including the seam allowance.)

2 Arrange these so that the light and dark triangles form a zigzag pattern around the outer edges of the quilt. Join the units together. In the quilt illustrated the chevron border is 2 units deep on 2 adjacent sides and 3 units deep on the other 2 sides, as shown in Figs 21 and 22. The corners are filled with squares cut 3½in (9cm). You can make the focus of the chevron light or dark. Refer to the photograph on page 30 as a guide.

3 Stitch the borders to the edges of the quilt. Press the seams.

Fig 21. Arrange the half-triangle units to create a chevron border 3 blocks deep to go around 2 sides of the quilt

Fig 22. Arrange half-triangle units to create a chevron border 2 blocks deep to go around the remaining sides of the quilt

Tip

Thread Dilemma

Monofilament (invisible) or variegated threads are good choices for machine quilting these multicoloured quilts.

Quilting the layers

1 Cut the wadding and the backing fabric so that they are 1½in (4cm) larger all round than the quilt top. Assemble the 3 layers of the quilt with the quilt top centred on the wadding, and the backing fabric underneath. Pin and then tack (baste) horizontal and vertical grid lines about 4in (10cm) apart across the entire quilt.

2 Quilt as desired by hand or machine (see page 116) using an appropriate quilting thread. Alternatively, enlist the services of a quilter with a long-arm quilting machine (see page 116). I machine quilted in zigzag lines using invisible monofilament thread and a walking foot on the machine. I did not try to quilt in parallel lines to the seams. Instead the zigzag lines were deliberately offset to make the quilting easy and overcome the necessity of marking the quilting lines.

Binding and finishing

1 Cut binding strips 2½in (6.25cm) wide, piecing them together as necessary to make up the required length.

2 Trim the wadding and backing fabrics a scant ¼in (0.75cm) beyond the edge of the quilt top.

3 Press the binding in half lengthways with wrong sides facing and attach it to the quilt following the instructions for straight binding with square corners on page 118.

4 Don't forget to add a label to the back of the quilt stating who made it and when plus any other information desired.

Galaxy of Stars and Scraps

Two lovely star blocks feature on this quilt: the Friendship Star and the Eight-Pointed Star. Notice how by arranging the star fabrics in different ways the two star blocks become many, many more – a veritable galaxy. I have made several versions of this quilt design and because of the wide variety of fabrics used and the way you can alter the blocks in a number of different ways they are always fun to work. And every quilt made using this formula is unique.

Beloved by quilters everywhere, star blocks provide an excuse to utilize bright colours that you might otherwise be fearful of using. Mine are made in eye-catching combinations of bright, light and dark fabrics. They are framed by the half-square triangle units made in scrap fabric, which appear as dark diamonds around the stars. When the blocks are stitched together a secondary design of light diamonds appears to link the stars together.

Galaxy of Stars and Scraps, 90 x 90in (229 x 229cm)
Quilted by Rosemary Archer of Frome Valley Quilting

Fabric Notes...

When people see my quilts they often comment 'you must have a vast collection of fabric'. Although I do have lots of different fabrics they are all fairly small pieces. I usually buy only quarter or half metre pieces from fabric shops. Having spent the last fifteen years travelling to teach, I have visited most of the quilt shops in the U.K. that have classrooms, so I can pick up unusual and appealing fabrics where and when I see them. The range of fabrics produced just for quilters are enormous now so we all have lots to choose from. My choices of fabric have probably become more adventurous as I progress; there was a time when I was not confident to use yellow or any bright colour. You can see by looking at the fabrics in this quilt that this is no longer the case.

Galaxy of Stars and Scraps. From two basic star blocks you can create all these variations for a dazzling scrap quilt

Galaxy of Stars and Scraps

Finished block
12 x 12in (30.5 x 30.5cm)
Finished quilt
90 x 90in (229 x 229cm)

Fabric requirements
Cotton fabric: for a double size quilt a total of 12 yards (11 metres) of fabric scraps in dark, light and bright patterned fabrics. Anything bigger than 4 and 5in (10 and 12.75cm) squares can be used
Binding: 1 yard (1 metre) of cotton fabric
Backing: cotton fabric(s) made up to 98 x 98in (249 x 249cm) square
Wadding: 98 x 98in (249 x 249cm) square

Assembly

Each block is 12in (30.5cm) square and features a central star surrounded by 12 half-square triangle units. You will need 49 blocks to make the quilt shown, arranged as 7 x 7. The border is created out of a single row of half-square triangle units.

Making the half-square triangle units

Each star is surrounded by a frame of half-square triangle units that create the dark frames and the secondary design of light diamonds. There is also a further border of half-square triangle units around the quilt. Begin by making some of these half-square triangle units. Ultimately you will need 704!

1 Cut squares $3\frac{7}{8}$in (10cm) from your scrap fabrics then pair them up in dark/light combinations and make up into half-square triangle units as directed on page 113. At this stage they will measure $3\frac{1}{2}$in (9cm) square.

2 For each block you will need 12 of these units, like the ones shown below. Make 24–36 as a start. These can be added to as you progress. Set these aside.

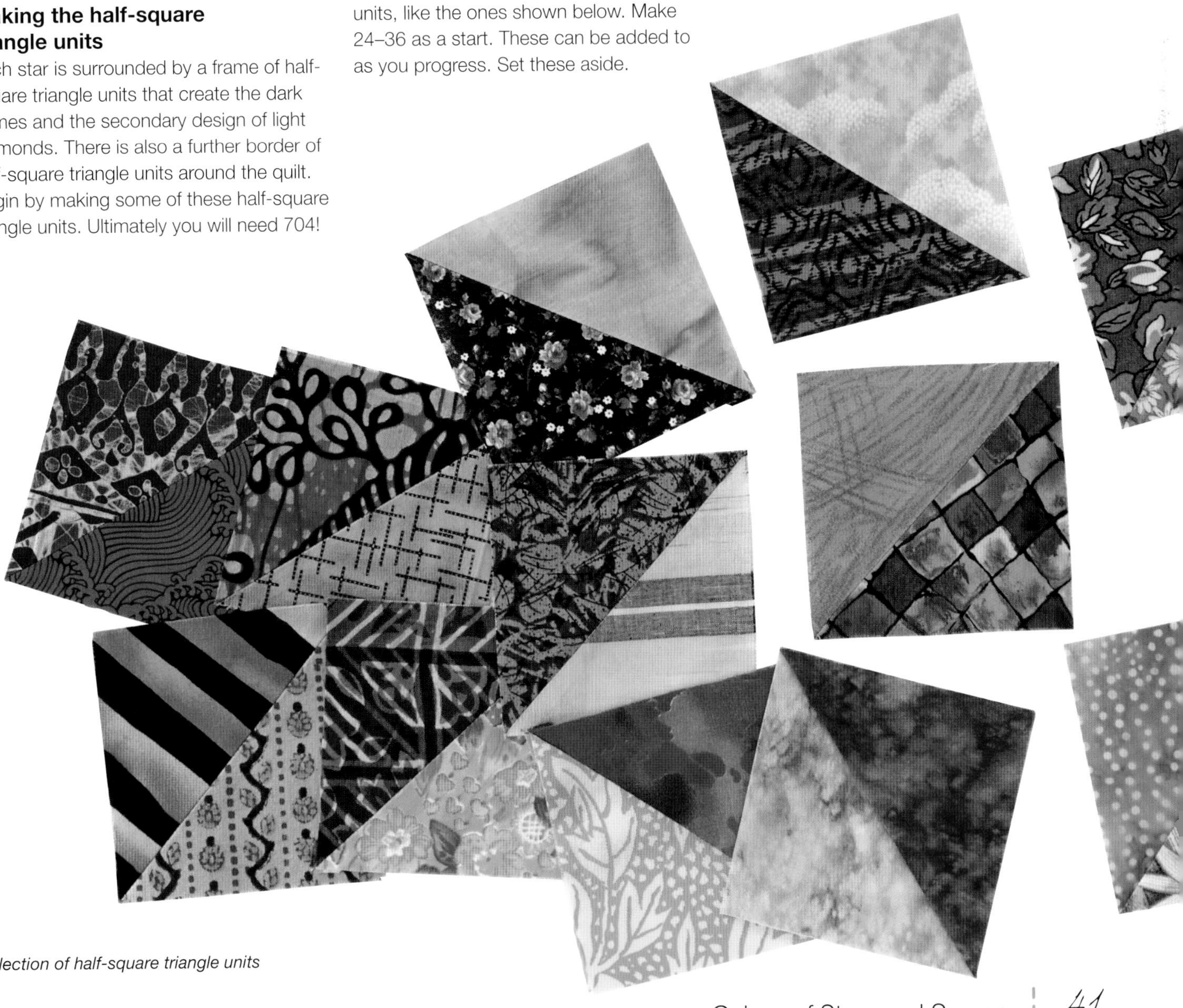

Selection of half-square triangle units

Making the Friendship Star block

This block (see Fig 1) is 6in (15.25cm) square and made from 2 fabrics which have a high contrast in either bright/dark or light/dark combinations. You will need 24 of these blocks for the quilt illustrated, including your variations (see right).

1 Decide which fabric is to be the star and which the background.

2 Study the block diagram in Fig 2, below, for the different shapes required. You will need 4 A squares in the background fabric and 1 in the star fabric. Cut these 2½in (6.5cm).

3 For the B triangle units you will need 2 pairs of squares in the contrasting fabrics. Cut these 2⅞in (7.25cm). From these make half-square triangle units as directed on page 113; 2 pairs of squares will yield 4 units.

4 Refer to Fig 3, below, to set out the squares and triangle units in the correct order. Stitch together in columns then join the columns as shown in the diagram.

5 Stitch half-square triangle units around each Friendship Star to complete the block, as shown in Fig 4.

Fig 1. Basic Friendship Star

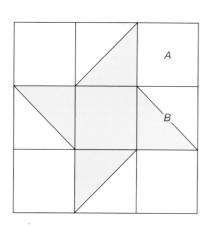

Fig 2. Refer to this block diagram to cut the Friendship Star fabrics

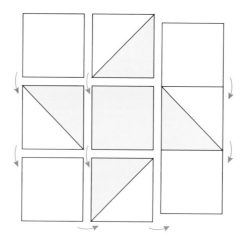

Fig 3. Assemble the units column by column then join the columns

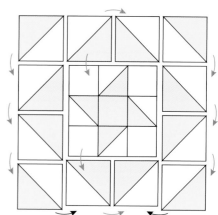

Fig 4. Add half-square triangle units around the Friendship Star to complete the block

Creating Variations of the Friendship Star Block

To give each of your Friendship Stars a different look, try the following variations:

1 Reverse the orientation of the seams in the B unit to make the star turn the other way, as shown in Fig 1.

2 Introduce a third fabric in the corners, as shown in Fig 2.

3 Make a diamond in a square for the centre of the block as shown in Fig 3. To do this cut the centre square 2½in (6.5cm). In the contrasting fabric cut four squares 1½in (4cm). Make a diamond in a square as explained on page 115.

4 Use quarter-square triangle units for a pieced centre as shown in Fig 4. Instead of the 2½in square centre, cut 1 square 3¼in (8.25cm) from each fabric. Place these right sides together and follow the instructions for making quarter-square triangle units on page 113. This will make 2 pieced centres. Set one aside for another block.

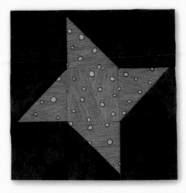

Fig 1. Try reversing the orientation of the seams in the B unit of the block so the star faces the other way

Fig 2. Use a third fabric for the corner units, as shown here

Fig 3. Make a diamond in a square for the centre of the block

Fig 4. Create a pieced centre using a quarter-square triangle unit

Quilt detail. When the blocks are assembled the light and dark tones form new patterns

Fig 5. Basic Eight-Pointed Star

Making the Eight-Pointed Star block

This block (Fig 5) is made from 2 fabrics that have a high contrast in either bright/dark or light/dark combinations. You will need 25 of these blocks in total including your variations (see below).

1 Decide which fabric is to be the star and which the background.

2 Study the block diagram in Fig 6 for the different pieces required. You will need 1 A square 3½in (9cm) in the star fabric for the block centre and 4 B squares 2in (5cm) in the background fabric for the corners of the block.

3 For the C units, which make up the star points, cut 1 background square 4¼in (10.75cm) and 4 squares of star fabric 2³⁄₈in (6cm).

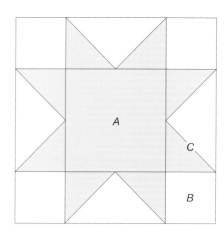

Fig 6. Refer to this block diagram to cut the Eight-Pointed Star fabrics

4 To make the C units follow the directions for making quick-pieced Flying Geese on page 114.

Creating Variations of the Eight-Pointed Star Block

To give each of your Eight-Pointed Star blocks a different look, try the following simple variations:

1 Use a third fabric for the centre of the star (A square) as in Fig 1, right.

2 Make a diamond in a square for the centre of the block as in Fig 2. To do this cut the centre A square from the star fabric. Now cut 4 squares 2in (5cm) from the background fabric. Make a diamond in a square as on page 115.

3 Make a variation of the diamond in a square, reversing the background and star fabrics (see Fig 3, right). Cut the A square in background fabric and the smaller squares in the star fabric.

4 Use quarter-square triangles for a pieced centre (see Fig 4). Cut 1 square of each fabric 4¼in (10.75cm). Place these right sides together and follow the instructions for making quarter-square triangles on page 113. This will make 2 pieced centres. Use one for another block.

Fig 1. Use a third fabric for the centre of the star (A square)

Fig 2. Make a diamond in a square for the centre of the block

Fig 3. Make a diamond in a square for the centre of the block with the background and star fabrics reversed

Fig 4. Make a quarter-square triangle block for the centre of the star as explained on page 113

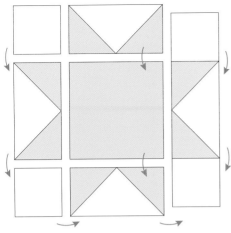

Fig 7. Assemble the units column by column then join the columns into the block

5 Assemble the units as shown in Fig 7, joining the units into columns (red arrows) and then joining the columns.

6 Complete the block by adding half-square triangle units around the edge in the same way as for the Friendship Star (see Fig 8, right).

Joining the blocks

Arrange the blocks together 7 across by 7 down, alternating the Eight-Pointed Star blocks with the Friendship Star blocks. Use a design wall if possible. Now stitch the blocks together.

Adding the border

1 Stitch half-square triangle units together in a line, placing the dark and light triangles to make a chevron pattern. Set these along the edges of the quilt top and join the strips to the centre panel so that the light diamonds are extended into the edges of the quilt. You will need 28 for the top and

Fig 8. Add half-square triangle units around the edge of the Eight-Pointed Star to complete the block

bottom and 30 for the 2 remaining sides, as shown in Fig 9.

2 Press and trim all threads away from the back and front of the quilt.

Quilting the layers

1 Cut the wadding and the backing fabric so that they are 1½in (4cm) larger all round than the quilt top. Assemble the 3 layers of the quilt with the quilt top centred on the wadding, and the backing fabric underneath. Pin and then tack (baste) horizontal and vertical grid lines about 4in (10cm) apart across the entire quilt.

2 Quilt as desired by hand or machine (see page 116) using an appropriate quilting thread. Alternatively, enlist the services of a quilter with a long-arm quilting machine (see page 116).

Binding and finishing

1 Cut binding strips 2½in (6.25cm) wide, piecing them together as necessary.

2 Trim the wadding and backing fabrics a scant ¼in (0.75cm) beyond the edge of the quilt top.

3 Press the binding in half lengthways with wrong sides facing and attach it to the quilt following the instructions for straight binding with square corners on page 118.

4 Don't forget to add a label to the back of the quilt stating who made it and when plus any other information desired.

Fig 9. Layout for the quilt blocks; note that this diagram shows 16 star blocks to give you an idea of the layout but your quilt will have 49

Galaxy of Stars and Scraps | 45

Dark Stars

Building on your library of stars, this quilt uses the two from the previous quilt plus a new one, the Ohio Star. To spice things up a bit, the blocks also come in two sizes and each star has variations, creating a delightfully complex effect. Instructions are provided for making the variations, but as you progress you will probably want to create your own.

Combining different sized blocks successfully is just a matter of thoughtful planning. In this case, three of the smaller blocks fit against two of the larger ones. This makes it interesting to construct, giving a mosaic-like effect, with plenty of scope for individual interpretation.

Dark Stars, 84 x 87in (213.25 x 221cm)
Quilted by Beryl Cadman of Custom Quilting

Fabric Notes...

For this quilt I selected a limited palette of blues, neutral and pink fabrics. I thought it was time I exercised more control over the fabrics and the original intention was to use just a range of blues, purples, turquoise and neutrals. As I worked on the blocks and quilt top though, it seemed to be a little bland and boring, so the pinks were introduced to add a bit of sparkle and interest. The 'Fossil Fern' range and 'Bali' batiks plus some Japanese prints form a large part of the fabric range in this quilt. For the lights I chose pale blues through to green, pastel grey and some beige fabrics including a rather nice calligraphic design.

Dark Stars. Distribute eye-catching fabrics, such as the pink and lime green over the surface of the quilt top to keep the eye moving

Dark Stars

Finished blocks
9 x 9in (23 x 23cm) and
6 x 6in (15.25 x 15.25cm)
Finished quilt
84 x 87in (213.25 x 221cm)

Fabric requirements
Cotton fabric: a total of 12 yards (11 metres) of fabric scraps in a range of blues, neutral, beige, grey and pink prints; floral, geometric batiks etc.
Binding: 1 yard (1 metre) of cotton fabric
Backing: cotton fabric(s) made up to 92 x 95in (233.5 x 241cm)
Wadding: Low-loft wadding 92 x 95in (233.5 x 241cm)

Assembly

Working with blocks in 2 sizes is made easier by joining them into larger units of 2 large Ohio Stars and 3 smaller Friendship Stars or Eight-Pointed Stars. For variation another unit is created with 1 Ohio Star, a smaller star and 2 square blocks.

Making the Ohio Star block

This block (Fig 1) is 9in (23cm) square. You will need a total of 42 for the quilt shown, including your variations (see page 50).

1 Referring to the block diagram in Fig 2, choose 2 contrasting dark/light fabrics. For the A squares cut 5 squares 3½in (9cm), 4 in light fabric for the corners and 1 dark fabric for the centre.

2 For the star point units (B) cut 2 squares 4¼in (10.75cm) of each fabric. Place these right sides together in pairs of 1 light and 1 dark fabric and make quarter-square triangle units as explained on page 113. Each pair of squares will make 2 units, so this will yield 4.

3 Arrange your squares on a flat surface and stitch the block together following the piecing sequence in Fig 3, below.

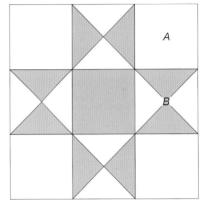

Fig 2. Block diagram

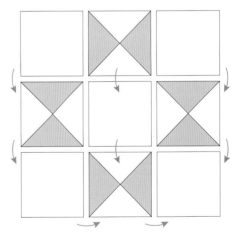

Fig 3. Piecing sequence for the Ohio Star block – join the squares into columns then join the columns

Fig 1. The Ohio Star block

Creating Variations of the Ohio Star Block

To give each of your Ohio Stars a different look, try the following variations:

1 Make half-square triangles for the corner squares. To do this, choose 2 fabrics. Cut 2 squares 3⁷⁄₈in (9.75cm) from each (4 squares altogether). Place these right sides together in pairs of 1 light and 1 dark and make half-square triangles as explained on page 113. When piecing the block, substitute these half-square units in the corners of the block, as shown in Fig 1, right.

2 Make a pieced centre using the technique for making quarter-squares triangle units used for the star points (B units). You can use the same 2 fabrics or introduce different fabrics as shown in Fig 2, right.

3 Make a diamond in a square for the centre. Cut the centre as a 3½in (9cm) square as for the basic block. Now, choosing a contrasting fabric, cut 4 squares 2in (5cm). Make a diamond in a square following the instructions on page 115.

4 For a completely different look, replace the corner squares with half-square triangles as in example 1 above and make a quarter-square triangle unit for the centre as in example 2. Careful placement of light and dark fabrics results in a new pattern of diamonds and rectangular blocks.

Fig 1. As a variation, make half-square triangles for the corner squares

Fig 2. For this variation of the Ohio Star make a quarter-square triangle unit as explained on page 113

Fig 3. Replace the plain central square with a diamond in a square, as explained left and on page 115

Fig 4. Use half-square triangle blocks in the corners and a quarter-square triangle block in the centre. Arrange the light and dark tones carefully to create this striking block design.

Making the Eight-Pointed Star block

This block (Fig 4) is 6in (15.25cm) square. You will need 1 or 2 for each set of blocks. Include some of the variations given on page 52.

1 Referring to the block diagram in Fig 5, choose 2 contrasting dark/light fabrics. Decide which is to be the star and which the background. For the A square (the centre) cut 1 square 3½in (9cm) from the star fabric. For the B squares (the corners) cut 4 squares 2in (5cm) from the background fabric.

2 For the C unit (star points) cut 1 square 4¼in (10.75cm) of background fabric and 4 squares 2³⁄₈in (6cm) of star fabric. Use the Quick-pieced Flying Geese technique described on page 114 to make the 4 star point units.

3 Arrange the A, B and C units on a flat surface following the order shown in Fig 6. Still referring to the diagram, stitch the block together in sequence. Stitch the seams marked with red arrows first to join the units into columns then join the columns as indicated by the green arrows.

Fig 4. Eight-Pointed Star block

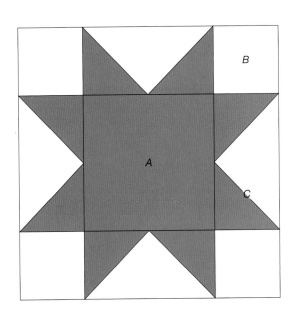

Fig 5. Block diagram

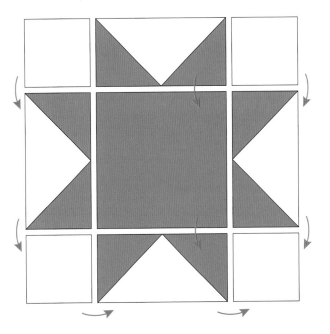

Fig 6. Piecing sequence for the Eight-Pointed Star block – join the squares into columns then join the columns

Creating Variations of the Eight-Pointed Star Block

To give each of your Eight-Pointed Star blocks a different look, try the following variations:

1 Cut the centre square from a different fabric for an easy variation, as shown in Fig 1, right.

2 Use a diamond in a square for the centre of the star (see Fig 2, right). Cut the centre square 3½in (8.75cm) from the star fabric. Now cut 4 squares 2in (5cm) in contrasting fabric and follow the sequence for making a Diamond in a Square on page 115.

3 Make a pieced centre of quarter-square triangles and, if desired, use half-square triangle blocks in the corners. For this centre cut 2 squares 4¼in (10.75cm) in contrasting fabrics. Place these right sides together and follow the procedure for making quarter-square triangles on page 113. For the corner squares choose 2 contrasting fabrics. Cut 2 2³⁄₈in (6cm) squares of each. Place these right sides together in pairs of 1 light and 1 dark and follow the procedure for making half-square triangles given on page 113.

4 Make a variation of the diamond in a square, reversing the background and star fabrics (see Fig 4, right). Cut the A square in background fabric and the smaller squares in the star fabric.

Fig 1. For a quick variation use a different fabric in the centre of the Eight-Pointed star block

Fig 2. For this variation replace the plain central unit with a diamond in a square

Fig 3. Replace the central square with a quarter-square triangle unit and the corners with half-square triangle units in this variation

Fig 4. Make a diamond in a square as in Fig 2, above, but reverse the star and background fabrics

Making the Friendship Star Block

This block (Fig 7, right) is 6in (15.25cm) square. You will need one or two for each set of blocks. Include some of the variations on page 54.

1 Referring to the block diagram, Fig 8, choose 2 contrasting fabrics, 1 for the star and 1 for the background. For the A squares cut 2½in (6.25cm) squares, 4 from the background fabric and 1 from the star fabric.

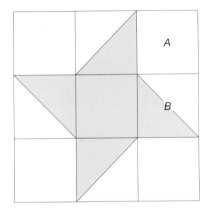

Fig 8. Block diagram

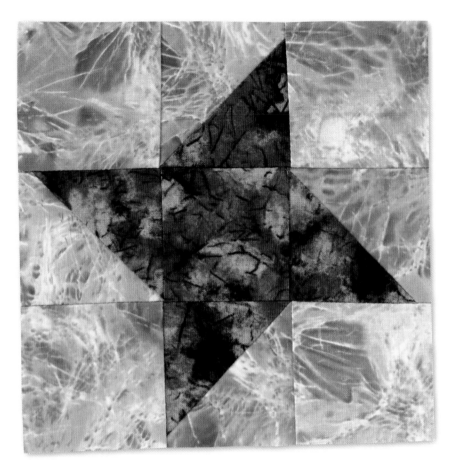

Fig 7. Friendship Star block

2 For the B units cut 2 squares 2⁷⁄₈in (7.25cm) from each fabric (4 squares altogether). Place these right sides together in pairs of 1 light and 1 dark and make half-square triangle units following the instructions on page 113.

3 Set out the pieces on a flat surface using Fig 9 as a guide. Still referring to the diagram, stitch the block together in sequence. Stitch the seams marked with red arrows first to join the units into columns, then join the columns as indicated by the green arrows.

Tip
Easy match

Matching points is easier if you cut accurately and maintain the ¼in (0.75cm) seam allowance carefully.

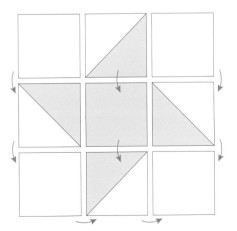

Fig 9. Piecing sequence for the Friendship Star block – join the squares into columns then join the columns

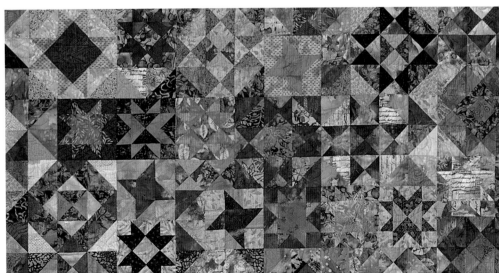

Creating Variations of the Friendship Star Block

To give each of your Friendship Star blocks a different look, try the following variations:

1 Use a third fabric for the centre of the star (Fig 1). If you wish, you can also reverse the direction of the seams on the B units to make the star rotate in the opposite direction, as shown in Fig 1, right.

2 Replace the central square with a quarter-square triangle unit. Cut 1 square of each fabric 3¼in (8.25cm). Place these right sides together and make quarter-square triangle units as explained on page 113.

3 Replace the central square with a diamond in a square. Cut the centre square from the star fabric 2½in (6.25cm). Cut 4 squares 1½in (4cm) from the background fabric. Make a diamond in a square as explained on page 115.

4 Make a variation of the diamond in a square in step 3, reversing the star and background fabrics for a whole new look.

Fig 1. As a variation, use a third fabric in the centre of the star. In this case the colour is similar to the main star fabric for a subtle effect

Fig 2. Make a quarter-square triangle block for the centre of the Friendship Star, as shown here

Fig 3. Make a diamond in a square for the centre of the Friendship Star

Fig 4. For a further variation, make a diamond in a square for the centre of the star but reverse the fabrics used

Creating larger blocks

1 When you have made 2 of the Ohio Star blocks and 3 Friendship Star blocks in any combination stitch the 2 Ohio Star blocks together, one above the other. Next join the 3 Friendship Star blocks in a column and join the columns together as in Fig 10.

2 If all the blocks were built up in the same way you would create long columns of Ohio Stars and similar columns of smaller stars. In order to avoid this, create a second large block with 1 Ohio Star on the other side. Join it to a Friendship Star block and fill in the gap with 2 square units, which can be plain squares, half-square triangle units or quarter-square triangle units as long as they are 3in (7.5cm) finished size.

3 Use a design wall to arrange the blocks as you work, making as many as you need for the desired size.

Tip

Change of scale

As an alternative to creating contrast with tonal values every time, try changing the scale of the patterns from small to large.

Adding the chevron border

The quilt is framed by a border of half-square triangle units arranged in a chevron pattern. Make up as many as you need for the size of your quilt. Stitch these together in strips and add to the top, bottom and sides of the quilt. The quilt illustrated would need 106 altogether. Refer to Fig 10 to see how the border joins onto the quilt. The corners are squares cut 3½in (9cm).

Quilting the layers

1 Cut the wadding and the backing fabric so that they are 1½in (4cm) larger all round than the quilt top. Assemble the 3 layers of the quilt with the quilt top centred on the wadding, and the backing fabric underneath. Pin and then tack (baste) horizontal and vertical grid lines about 4in (10cm) apart across the entire quilt.

2 Quilt as desired by hand or machine (see page 116) using an appropriate quilting thread. Alternatively, enlist the services of a quilter with a long-arm quilting machine (see page 116).

Binding and finishing

1 Cut binding strips 2½in (6.25cm) wide, piecing them together as necessary to make up the required length.

2 Trim the wadding and backing fabrics a scant ¼in (0.75cm) beyond the edge of the quilt top.

3 Press the binding in half lengthways with wrong sides facing and attach it to the quilt following the instructions for straight binding with square corners on page 118.

4 Don't forget to add a label to the back of the quilt stating who made it and when plus any other information desired.

Fig 10. Layout for the quilt blocks

Dark Stars | *55*

Splashes of Colour

Sizzling with colour and pattern, this spectacular quilt draws energy
from the myriad triangles in several sizes that seem to move and
change before your eyes like sunlight playing on a garden of flowers.
The exciting combination of colours is like an explosion of joy.

Each block in this quilt is a union between a large triangle and a pieced triangle,
creating a striking diagonal focus on the finished quilt. The large triangles provide
areas of comparative rest for the eye and enable you to progress more quickly,
while the pieced triangles are where the excitement lies. These enable you to
use up some of your smaller scraps and are not as difficult to make as they look.

Splashes of Colour, 64 x 64in (162.5 x 162.5cm)
Quilted by Rosemary Archer of Frome Valley Quilting

Fabric Notes...

For the small triangles I cut high-contrast fabrics in a wide variety of colours. These give the
quilt energy and movement highlighted by the bright oranges, yellows and pinks. Orange fabrics
are also used in the large triangles to echo this and give the quilt a warm glow. Many patterned
fabrics are put together, with both large and small prints, and these are contained by a broad
binding of dark grey.

Splashes of Colour. There is plenty of interest in both the fabrics and the design to make either a wall hanging or a bed quilt that would enhance any interior

Splashes of Colour

Finished block
8 x 8in (20.25 x 20.25cm)
Finished quilt
64 x 64in (162.5 x 162.5cm)

Fabric requirements
Cotton fabric: a total of 5½ yards (5 metres) of fabric scraps in dark and light patterned fabrics
Binding: ¾ yard (0.75 metre) of cotton fabric
Backing: cotton fabric(s) made up to 72 x 72in (183 x 183cm)
Wadding: 72 x 72in (183 x 183cm)

Assembly

Each block is made from triangles in three sizes plus a square, but provided that you cut and stitch accurately, assemble is straightforward. You will need 64 blocks for the quilt shown.

Cutting the fabrics for the blocks

1 Refer to the letters on the block diagram to select and cut the fabrics for each block. Begin with the A units, which are comprised of 2 right-angled triangles. Cut out 2⅞in (7.25cm) squares in a variety of values and patterns. Place these right sides together in contrasting pairs and make half-square triangle units following the instructions on page 113. Press the seams to the darker side and snip off the extending seam allowances. Make 20–30 of these to start with then add more as you progress. Altogether you will need 256 units.

2 For the D triangles cut the same size squares – 2⅞in (7.25cm) – then cut across 1 diagonal to make the triangles. You will need 128 altogether and its best to cut them as you go along. These can be in both light and dark fabrics.

3 For the B triangle, cut squares 4⅞in (12.5cm) and divide these into 2 triangles by cutting across 1 diagonal. There is 1 for each block so you will need 64 altogether cut from 32 squares.

4 For the E squares cut 2½in (6.25cm) squares in both lights and darks. There is 1 in each block so you will need 64.

5 For the C triangles cut an 8⅞in (22.5cm) square of paper then cut this across 1 diagonal to create a template. This ensures you will not have repeats of the same fabric in the large triangles. If preferred, you can cut the squares from fabric and divide these across 1 diagonal to make 2 C triangles.

Tip
Tonal variation

If the unpieced C triangles seem too bold when you are piecing the blocks, remember that the quilting will add texture and break up the blank areas.

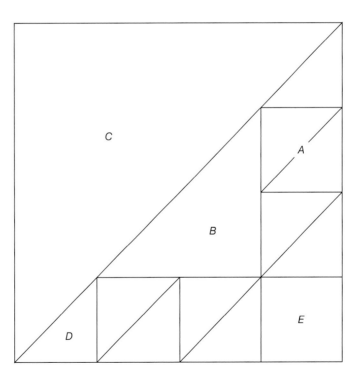

Fig 1. Block diagram

Making the blocks

1 Referring to Fig 1 again, lay out 1 C triangle, 1 B triangle, 2 D triangles, 1 E square and 4 A units. Keep a good contrast between the pieces. Depending on the value of the B triangle, you can put either the dark or the light fabrics in the A units next to it.

2 Now join the pieces together. Start by joining a D triangle to an A unit; join the A unit to a second A unit and then join this to the E square. Now join the remaining D triangle to 2 A units, as shown in Fig 2.

3 Referring to Fig 3, right, join the shorter unit to one side of your B triangle, then join the longer unit to the adjacent side of the triangle and the attached A unit.

4 Finally, join your pieced triangle to the C triangle (Fig 4). Press the seams as you go. A completed block is shown in Fig 5.

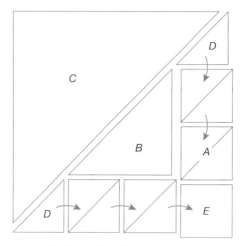

Fig 2. Join the D triangles to the A units and E square

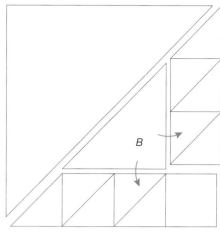

Fig 3. Attach the B triangle

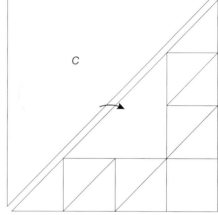

Fig 4. Join the pieced triangle to the C triangle

Joining the blocks

1 The quilt illustrated on page 58 has 64 blocks. Make all your blocks, cutting out and stitching more of the smaller pieces as you work.

2 Stitch blocks together in sets of 4, as shown in Fig 6, opposite.

3 Arrange your blocks of 4, using a design wall, if possible. When you are happy with the result, stitch the blocks together into 4 sections then stitch these together to complete the quilt top. This will avoid too many long seams.

Fig 5. The finished block

Quilting the layers

1 Cut the wadding and the backing fabric so that they are 2–3in (5–7.5cm) larger all round than the quilt top to accommodate broad binding. Assemble the 3 layers of the quilt with the quilt top centred on the wadding, and the backing fabric underneath. Pin and then tack (baste) horizontal and vertical grid lines about 4in (10cm) apart across the entire quilt.

2 Quilt as desired by hand or machine (see page 116) using an appropriate quilting thread. Another option is to enlist the services of a quilter who operates a long-arm quilting machine (see page 116 for advice).

Binding and finishing

1 Cut binding strips 5in (12.5cm) wide, piecing them together to make up the required length with extra for mitres.

2 Trim the backing and wadding to extend 1in (2.5cm) beyond the edges of the quilt.

3 Press the binding in half lengthways with wrong sides facing and attach it to the quilt following the instructions for broad binding with stitched mitres on page 119.

4 Don't forget to add a label to the back of the quilt stating who made it and when plus any other information desired.

Fig 6. A group of 4 blocks

Sampler Quilt

With literally hundreds of stunning block designs out there it can be difficult to decide between them. This is where the sampler quilt comes in, enabling you to make many different blocks and display them in a single quilt. Take the opportunity for some creativity by introducing your own favourites – you can swap any of the blocks provided that they are the same size.

For added colour and movement I have skewed the blocks and replaced the usual plain sashing with a saw-tooth pattern. An outer border of saw-tooth triangles on a slightly larger scale frames the quilt and, through its change of scale, draws the viewer in towards the centre of the quilt.

Sampler Quilt, 52½ x 52½in (133.5 x 133.5cm)
Quilted by the author

Fabric Notes...

When this quilt was made I had a large collection of 'Bali' batiks, most of which found their way into the block Teamed with these are hand-dyed and marbled fabrics with just a few prints. When it was started I did not rea have an idea of how it would look when finished. Select a wide variety of colours that will harmonize – small pieces from the scrap bag can be used along with some larger pieces and selected fat quarters. It is importar to use fabrics that contrast well to show up the block designs. In the pattern instructions for the blocks the fabrics are classified by colour and tone as a guide. Colours have been specified to match the quilt and for ea of explanation but you can use your own colours, if desired.

Sampler Quilt. As with other quilts in this collection, yellow is one of the key fabrics for providing focus points across the surface

Sampler Quilt

Finished block
6 x 6in (15.25 x 15.25cm);
9 x 9in (23 x 23cm) with tilted frame

Finished quilt
52½ x 52½in (133.5 x 133.5cm)

Fabric requirements
Cotton fabric: a total of 4½–5½ yards (4–5 metres)
Binding: 1½ yards (1.5 metres) of cotton fabric
Backing: cotton fabric(s) made up to 60 x 60in (154 x 154cm)
Wadding: 60½ x 60½in (154 x 154cm)

Assembly

There are 16 different blocks in this quilt. Instructions are given block by block, giving you the chance to alter the order as desired or introduce your own blocks. It is important to cut accurately and maintain a ¼in (0.75cm) seam allowance throughout. Refer to the block diagrams to help with cutting and piecing.

NB In these diagrams the shapes (squares or triangles) and units (2 or more pieced shapes) are labelled with letters for easy identification.

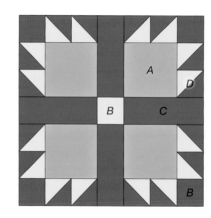

Fig 1. Block diagram

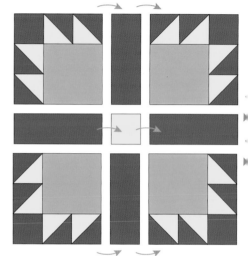

Fig 3. Joining the units to make the block

Making the Bear's Paw block

1 Choose three fabrics: yellow (bright), orange (medium) and green (dark). Refer to the block diagram in Fig 1, above right, to cut the following:

• 4 orange squares 2¼in (5.75cm) A

• 4 green square 1⅜in (3.5cm) and one yellow square 1⅜in (3.5cm) B

• For the C rectangles 4 green rectangles 3⅛ x 1⅜in (8 x 3.5cm)

2 For the half-square triangle units (D) cut 8 squares 1¾in (4.5cm) each in green and yellow. Place these right sides together in pairs of 1 green and 1 yellow and make half-square triangle units as explained on page 113.

3 Make the 4 paw units by joining D units together in pairs. Join 1 pair to each A square. Join the remaining pairs to a green B square and attach to the A square as shown in Fig 2, below.

4 Join the paw units together in pairs with a C rectangle between them. Join the remaining C rectangles with the yellow B square between them. Finally, join the pairs of paws together with the remaining strip in the middle, as shown in Fig 3, above.

Tip
Perfect pressing

When pressing seams I press the first set to the darker side of the fabrics then subsequent seams open. This will give a flatter appearance to the blocks but I recommend that you do what is comfortable for you when pressing seams.

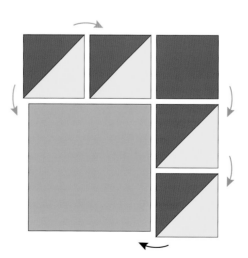

Fig 2. Making the paw units

Making the Pigeon Toes block

1 Choose 3 fabrics: yellow (bright), blue (dark) and green (medium). Refer to the block diagram to cut the following:

• For the centre A square 1 green square 3½in (9cm)

• 4 green squares 2in (5cm) B

2 For the half-square triangle units (C) cut 4 yellow and 4 blue squares 2⅜in (6cm). Place these right sides together in pairs of 1 blue and 1 yellow and make half-square triangle units as explained on page 113.

3 Join 4 C units together in pairs and stitch a pair to opposite sides of the A square, as shown in Fig 5. Take care to get the orientation of the seams correct.

4 Stitch the corner squares to the remaining C units and attach these to the centre panel, as shown in Fig 6.

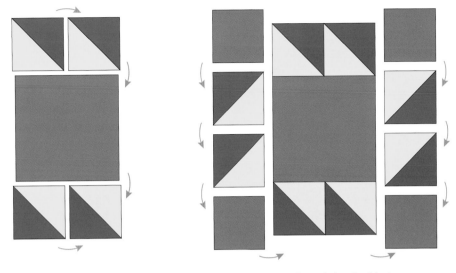

Fig 5. Join four half-square triangle units to the centre square

Fig 6. Completing the block

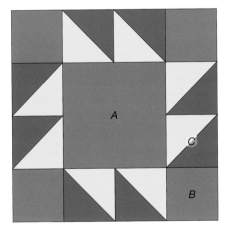

Fig 4. Block diagram

Making the Windmill block

1 Choose 5 fabrics: blue (dark), green (dark), orange (bright), grey (light) and brown (medium). Refer to the block diagram (Fig 7) to cut 4 grey squares 2in (5cm) A.

2 For the half-square triangle units (B) cut 4 blue, 2 orange, 2 brown, 2 green and 2 grey squares 2⅜in (6cm). Pair up the squares with 2 each of the following combinations: blue/brown, blue/orange, green/grey. Place these pairs right sides together and make half-square triangle units following the instructions on page 113.

3 Make the centre pinwheel using the blue/orange B units by joining your 4 units together as shown in Fig 8.

4 Join an A square to a green/grey B unit twice; stitch these to opposite sides of centre pinwheel. These are shown above and below the pinwheel in Fig 9.

5 Referring Fig 9, stitch the remaining units to the A squares to make the left- and right-hand columns. Join these to the centre panel to complete the block.

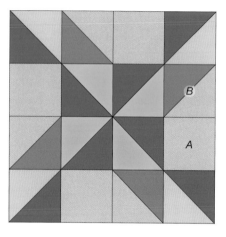

Fig 7. Block diagram

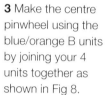

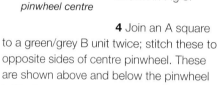

Fig 8. Making the pinwheel centre

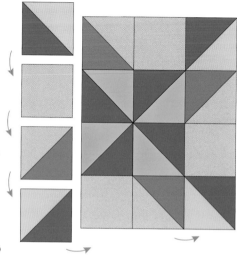

Fig 9. Completing the block

Making the Ohio Star block

1 Choose 3 fabrics: yellow (bright), maroon (dark) and ochre (medium). Refer to the block diagram shown in Fig 10 to cut 1 ochre square 2½in (6.25cm) and 4 maroon squares 2½in (6.25cm) A.

2 For the quarter-square triangle units (B) cut 2 yellow squares 3¼in (8.25cm) and 2 maroon squares 3¼in (8.25cm).

3 Place the 3¼in (8.25cm) squares right sides together in pairs of 1 yellow and 1 maroon square, and make quarter-square triangle units as explained on page 113.

4 Arrange the squares and units in the correct order and stitch them together in columns first then join the columns to complete the block as shown in Fig 12.

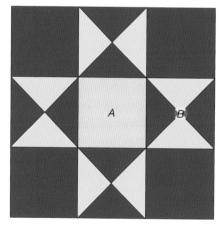

Fig 10. Block diagram

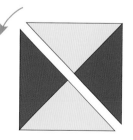

Fig 11. Make quarter-square triangle units

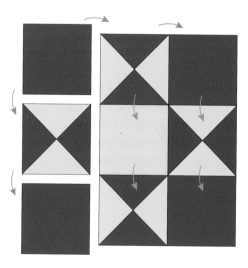

Fig 12. Joining the squares and units to complete the blocks

Making the King's Crown block

1 Choose 2 fabrics: red (bright) and navy blue (dark). Refer to the block diagram in Fig 13 to cut 4 navy blue squares 2in (5cm) A.

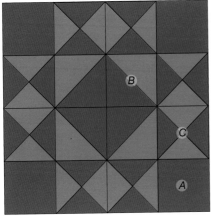

Fig 13. Block diagram

2 For the half-square triangle units (B) cut 2 red squares 2⅜in (6cm) and 2 navy squares 2⅜in (6cm). Place these right sides together in pairs of 1 red and 1 navy and make half-square triangle units following the instructions on page 113.

3 For the quarter-square triangle units (C) cut 4 navy squares 2¾in (7cm) and 4 red squares 2¾in (7cm). Place these right sides together in pairs of 1 navy and 1 red square and make quarter-square triangle units following the instructions on page 113. This will make 8 C units.

4 Referring to Fig 14, right, stitch 4 B units together to make the centre of the block, then stitch together 2 pairs of C units and add these to the top and bottom.

Fig 14. Making the centre panel and joining four C units

5 Stitch the remaining C units and A squares together in 2 columns as shown in Fig 15. Add these to the centre panel to complete the block.

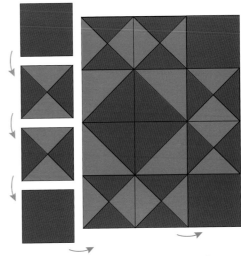

Fig 15. Completing the block

Making the Eight-Pointed Star block

1 Choose 2 fabrics: navy blue (dark) and pink (bright). Refer to the block diagram to cut the following:

• 1 pink square 3½in (3cm) A

• 4 navy blue squares 2in (5cm) B

2 For the star point units (C) cut 1 navy blue square 4¼in (10.75cm) and 4 pink squares 2⅜in (6cm) and follow the directions for making quick-pieced Flying Geese on page 114.

3 Referring to the block diagram in Fig 16, lay out your units in block order. Stitch them together in columns then join the columns to complete the block, as shown in Fig 17, right.

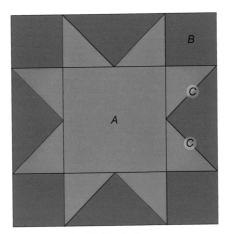

Fig 16. Block diagram

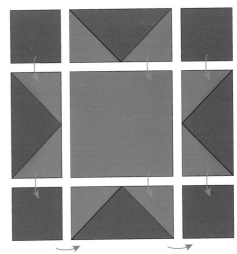

Fig 17. Joining the squares and units to make the block

Making the Double Star block

1 Choose 3 fabrics: yellow (bright), turquoise (medium) and red (dark). Refer to the block diagram in Fig 18 to cut 8 turquoise squares 1½in (3.75cm) A.

2 For the half-square triangle units (B) cut 8 red, 10 yellow and 10 turquoise squares 1⅞in (4.75cm) – 28 in total. Pair up the squares as follows:

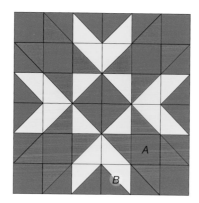

Fig 18. Block diagram

- red/turquoise 4 pairs
- red/yellow 4 pairs
- yellow/turquoise, 6 pairs

3 Place these pairs right sides together and make half-square triangle units following the instructions on page 113. This will yield 8 red/turquoise units, 8 red/yellow units and 12 yellow/turquoise units.

4 Referring to the block diagram, lay out the A squares and B units in the correct order. Stitch 6 vertical columns then stitch these together to complete the block, as shown in Fig 19.

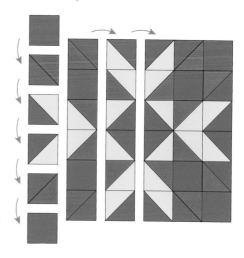

Fig 19. Joining the squares and units

Making the Pinwheel Quarto block

1 Choose 3 fabrics: yellow (bright), maroon (dark) orange (medium). Refer to the block diagram in Fig 20 to cut the following:

- 1 maroon square 1¾in (4.5cm) A
- 4 orange rectangles 1¾ x 3in (4.5 x 7.5cm) B

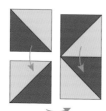

Fig 21. Making the pinwheels

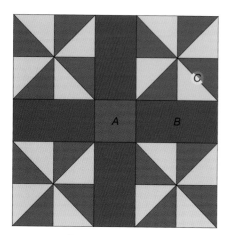

Fig 20. Block diagram

2 For the half-square triangle units (C) cut 8 yellow squares 2⅛in (5.5cm) and 8 maroon squares 2⅛in (5.5cm). Place these right sides together in pairs of 1 yellow and 1 maroon square and make half-square triangle units following the instructions on page 113.

3 Join the C units in groups of 4, as shown in Fig 21, to make four pinwheels.

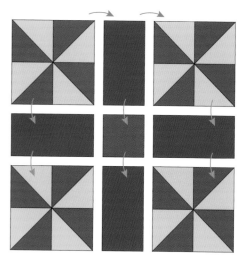

Fig 22. Joining the pieces and pinwheel units to make the block

4 Join the pinwheels in pairs with an orange rectangle B between each one. Join the remaining rectangles together with the maroon A square in between. Join the sets together with the A square in the middle, as shown, to complete the block.

Making the Diamond Pinwheel block

1 Choose 3 fabrics: pink (bright), green (medium) and navy blue (dark), referring to the block diagram in Fig 23. For the half-square triangles (A) cut 2 squares 3⅞in (10cm) in navy blue. Cut these across one diagonal to make four triangles.

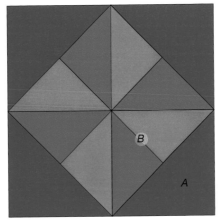

Fig 23. Block diagram

2 For the quarter-square triangle units (B) cut 1 pink square 4¼in (10.75cm) and 1 green square 4¼in (10.75cm). Place these right sides together and make 4 bi-coloured triangles following the instructions for making quarter-square triangles on page 113.

3 Stitch 1 pieced B triangle to each corner A triangle, then stitch these together to complete the block, as shown in Fig 24.

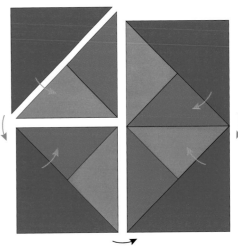

Fig 24. Joining the triangle units to the matching triangles to make the block

Making the Double Pinwheel block

1 Choose 3 fabrics: yellow (light), grey (dark) and pink (medium), referring to the block diagram in Fig 25. For the half-square triangles (A) cut 2 pink squares 3⅞in (10cm). Cut these across 1 diagonal to make 4 triangles.

2 For the quarter-square triangle units (B) cut 2 yellow squares 3⅜in (8.5cm) and 2 grey squares 3⅜in (8.5cm). Place these right sides together in pairs of 1 yellow and 1 grey square and make quarter-square triangle units following the instructions on page 113.

3 Stitch these units together in pairs, then join into a square, as shown in Fig 26.

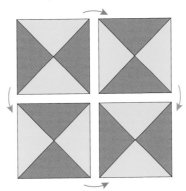

Fig 26. Joining the quarter-square triangle units

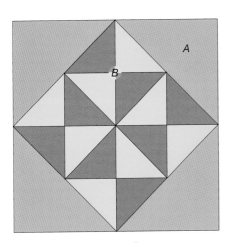

Fig 25. Block diagram

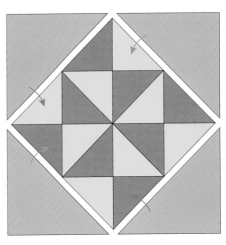

Fig 27. Adding the A triangles to complete the block

4 Turn this square on point and complete the block by stitching the A triangles to the 4 sides of the pinwheel, working in opposite pairs, as shown in Fig 27, above.

Making the Fancy Star block

1 Choose 3 fabrics: navy blue (dark), yellow (light) and orange (medium). Refer to the block diagram (Fig 28) to cut the following:

• 1 orange square 3½in (9cm) and 4 navy blue squares 1½in (3.75cm) for the central snowball unit A

• 4 orange squares 2in (5cm) for the corners (B)

• 1 orange square 4¼in (10.75cm) and 4 navy blue squares 1½in (3.75cm) for the large pieced triangle units (C)

• 2 yellow and 2 navy blue squares 2¾in (7cm) for the D units

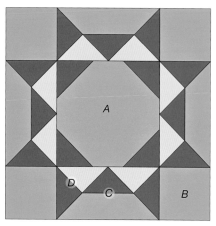

Fig 28. Block diagram

2 To make the snowball centre place 2 of the 1½in (3.75cm) navy blue squares at opposite corners of the 3½in (9cm) orange square with right sides together and corners matching. Mark diagonal lines on the blue squares and stitch on these lines, as shown in Fig 29. Cut away the corners ¼in (0.75cm) beyond the stitching.

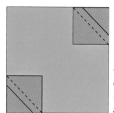

Fig 29. Join 2 small navy squares to the large orange A square

Fig 30. Join the other two small navy squares to the large orange A square

3 Press the navy blue corners over. Repeat with the remaining 2 navy blue squares as shown in Fig 30.

Fig 31. The finished snowball unit

4 Give the centre panel a final press to complete the snowball (Fig 31).

5 Now make the C units. Cut the 4¼in (10.75cm) orange square across both diagonals to make four triangles.

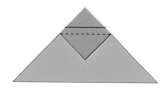

Fig 32. Piecing the C unit

6 Place 1 of the 1½in (3.75cm) navy blue squares over the right angle of 1 orange triangle with right sides facing and corners matching. Draw a diagonal line on the blue square and stitch along it as shown in Fig 32. Trim away the corner ¼in (0.75cm) beyond the stitching.

Fig 33. The finished C unit

7 Press the smaller triangle over, as shown in Fig 33. Repeat 3 more times to make 4 C units in total.

Fig 34. Stitching the D units

8 To make the D units place the 2¾in (7cm) squares right sides together in pairs of 1 blue and 1 yellow square. Mark 2 diagonal lines and stitch as shown in Fig 34.

9 Cut right across both diagonals and press. This will yield triangles with the correct colour placement.

Fig 35. Joining the C and D units

10 Stitch the C and D units together to make 4 star point units, as shown in Fig 35, above.

11 Referring to the block diagram in Fig 28, lay out the squares and units. Join them together in columns then join the columns together to complete the block as shown in Fig 36, below.

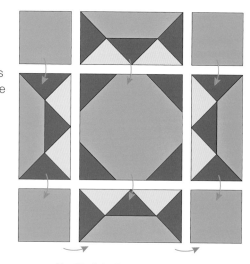

Fig 36. Join the squares and units to complete the block

Making the Dutchman's Puzzle block

1 Choose 3 fabrics: pink (medium), green (medium) and grey (light). Refer to the block diagram in Fig 37 to cut 8 grey squares 2⅜in (6cm). For the larger triangles cut 1 pink square 4¼in (10.75cm) and 1 green square 4¼in (10.75cm).

2 Use the pink square and 4 grey squares to make quick-pieced Flying Geese units, following the instructions on page 114. Repeat with the green square and remaining grey squares. You will have 8 units altogether.

Fig 37. Block diagram

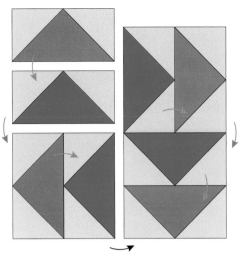

Fig 38. Join the Flying Geese unit to make the block

3 Referring to the block diagram (Fig 37), arrange the Flying Geese units in block order. Stitch the units together in pairs, join the pairs together and then join the two sets as shown in Fig 38.

Making the Complex Diamond block

1 Choose 3 fabrics: yellow (light), red (medium) and grey (dark). Refer to the block diagram in Fig 39 to cut the following:

- 1 grey square 2½in (6.25cm) A

- 1 yellow square 3¼in (8.25cm) cut across both diagonals to make 4 triangles B

- 2 red squares 2⅞in (7.25cm) cut across 1 diagonal to make 4 triangles C

- 1 red square 3¼in (8.25cm) and 4 grey squares 1⅞in (4.75cm) for the Flying Geese units D

- 6 squares 1⅞in (4.75cm) in yellow and 6 squares 1⅞in (4.75cm) in grey for the half-square triangle units E

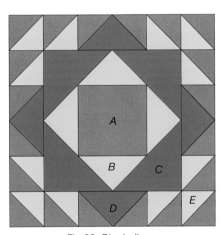

Fig 39. Block diagram

2 Sew the 4 yellow B triangles to the grey centre A square working in opposite pairs, as shown in Fig 40.

3 Add a red C triangle to each edge of your pieced square, as shown in Fig 41, again working in opposite pairs.

4 Using the red squares 3¼in (8.25cm) and the 4 grey squares 1⅞in (4.75cm) make quick-pieced Flying Geese units following the instructions on page 114. These are your D units.

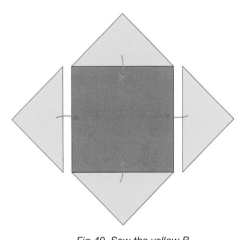

Fig 40. Sew the yellow B triangles to the grey A square

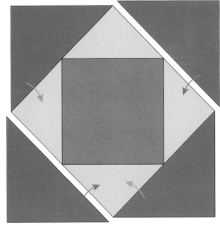

Fig 41. Attach the red C triangles

Sampler Quilt | 71

5 For the E units place the yellow and grey squares 1⅞in (4.5cm) right sides together in pairs and make 12 bi-coloured squares following the instructions for making half-square triangle units on page 113.

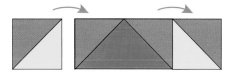

Fig 42. Attach two E units to a D unit

6 Stitch 1 E unit to each end of a D unit, as shown in Fig 42; repeat.

7 Add these new units to opposite sides of the centre square (Fig 43).

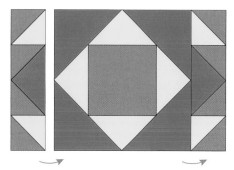

Fig 43. Join your units to the central pieced square

8 Referring to the block diagram in Fig 39 for colour placement, stitch two E units to each end of the remaining D units. Add these to the top and bottom of the panel to complete the block, as shown in Fig 44.

Fig 44. Completing the block

Making Martha Washington's Star block

1 Choose 4 fabrics: blue (dark), grey (light), yellow (bright) and brown (dark). Refer to the block diagram to cut the following:

• 1 brown and 1 yellow square 2¾in (7cm) and 2 blue squares 2⅜in (6cm) for the pinwheel centre (A)

• 4 grey squares 2in (5cm) for the corner squares (B)

• 1 grey square 4¼in (10.75cm) and 4 blue squares 2⅜in (6cm) for the Flying Geese units (C)

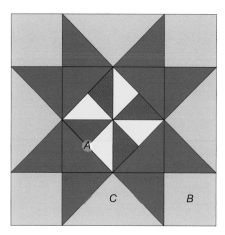

Fig 45. Block diagram

2 Place the 2¾in (7cm) brown and yellow squares right sides together and make 4 bi-coloured triangles following the instructions for making quarter-square triangle units on page 113.

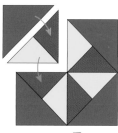

Fig 46. Making the central pinwheel (A)

3 Cut the 2 blue squares 2⅜in (6cm) across 1 diagonal to make 4 triangles. Pair these triangles with the bi-coloured triangles and stitch together. Join the squares to complete the central pinwheel, as shown in Fig 46.

3 Use the grey square 4¼in (10.75cm) and the 4 blue squares 2⅜in (6cm) to make quick-pieced Flying Geese following the instructions on page 114. You should have 4 C units.

4 Referring to the block diagram in Fig 45, arrange the squares and units in the block. Stitch a B square on each end of 2 C units and a C unit on each end of the central pinwheel (A). Then join the resulting columns together to complete the block, as shown in Fig 47.

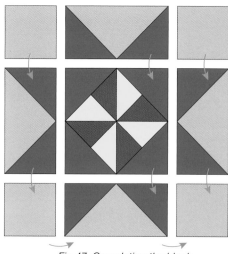

Fig 47. Completing the block

Making the Cross & Crown block

1 Choose 3 fabrics: orange (light), green (medium) and blue (dark). Refer to the block diagram in Fig 48 to cut the following:

• 2 orange squares 3⅜in (8.5cm) and 4 blue squares 1⅝in (4cm) for the A triangles

• 2 orange squares 2½in (6.25cm) and 2 green squares 2½in (6.25cm) for the B triangles

• 4 green rectangles 1¾ x 3in (3.75 x 7.5cm) C

• 4 green corner squares 1¾in (4.5cm) D and 1 blue square 1¾in (4.5cm) for the centre E

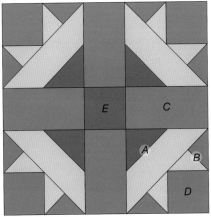

Fig 48. Block diagram

Fig 49. Adding the blue fabric to the orange A triangles

2 Divide the orange squares 3⅜in (8.5cm) across 1 diagonal to make 4 triangles. Place 1 of the blue squares 1⅝in (4cm) over an orange triangle with right sides together and corners aligned. Draw a diagonal line across the blue square and stitch on that line, as shown in Fig 49.

3 Trim off the corner ¼in (0.75cm) away from the stitching and press the small blue triangle over. Repeat 3 more times to make the 4 A units.

Fig 50. Stitching the B units

4 Place the 2½in (6.25cm) squares in orange/green pairs right sides together. Mark 2 diagonal lines and stitch as shown in Fig 50. Cut right across both diagonals. This will yield triangles with the correct colour placement for the B units.

5 Stitch 2 B units to adjacent sides of each green D square as shown in Fig 51, right.

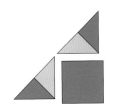

Fig 51. Adding the B units to the D squares

Fig 52. Joining the A unit to the B/D unit

6 Stitch the A units to the B/D units, as shown in Fig 52.

7 Referring to the block diagram in Fig 48, lay out the units, C rectangles and central square (E) in block order. Stitch the pieces together in columns as indicated by the red arrows in Fig 53, below, then join the columns to make the block, as indicated by the green arrows.

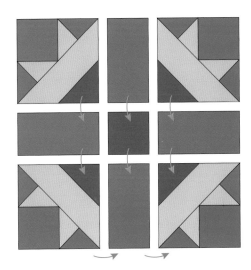

Fig 53. Completing the block

Tip
Handle with care

Bias edges, such as those across the triangles, will stretch and distort easily so handle them carefully to avoid pulling them out of shape.

Making the Broken Dishes block

1 Choose 3 fabrics: pink (medium), grey (dark) and yellow (light). Refer to the block diagram in Fig 54 to cut the following:

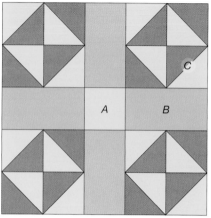

Fig 54. Block diagram

- 1 yellow square 1¾in (4.5cm) A

- 4 pink rectangles 1¾ x 3in (4.5 x 7.5cm) B

- 8 grey squares 2⅛in (5.5cm) and 8 yellow squares 2⅛in (5.5cm) for the pieced blocks C

2 Place the 2⅛in (5.5cm) squares right sides together in grey/yellow pairs and make half-square triangle units following the instructions on page 113.

3 Join the yellow/grey half-square triangle units into blocks of 4 as shown in Fig 55 to make the C units.

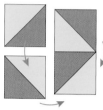

Fig 55. Making the pieced units

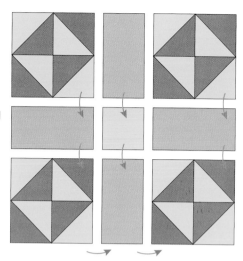

Fig 56. Completing the block

4 Referring to the block diagram in Fig 54, lay out the units, rectangles and central square in block order. Stitch them together in columns as indicated by the red arrows in Fig 56, then join the columns to complete the block.

Tilting the blocks

1 Cut 3in (7.5cm) wide strips of fabric to border the blocks. These can be cut from scraps and can be made using more than 1 fabric for each block. Refer to the picture on page 63 as a guide for fabric choices. Stitch these strips to all 4 sides of each block.

2 Cut a 9in (22.75cm) square template from tracing paper. Pin the paper to a block, tilting the paper square so that one corner touches each edge, as shown in Fig 57. Japanese flower pins are useful here because they will lie flat under your ruler. Trim around the paper using a ruler and rotary cutter for a clean cut.

3 Repeat on the remaining blocks, tilting 8 blocks in one direction, as shown in Fig 58, then tilting 8 blocks in the opposite direction, as shown in Fig 59.

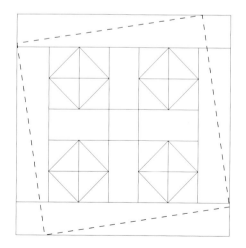

Fig 57. Use a square of tracing paper to cut the block on a tilt

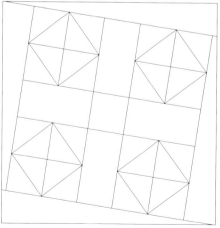

Fig 58. Tilt eight blocks in one direction

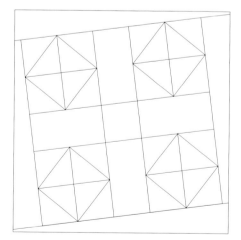

Fig 59. Tilt eight blocks in the opposite direction, as shown

Making the sashing between the blocks

1 For the saw-tooth sashing strips that separate the blocks cut 2½in (6.25cm) squares from scraps. Begin with about 20 or so different fabrics and add to them as you work.

2 Put the squares right sides together in light/dark pairs and make half-square triangle units following the instructions on page 113.

Bear's Paw	King's Crown	Diamond Pinwheel	Complex Diamond
Pigeon Toes	Eight-Pointed Star	Double Pinwheel	Martha Washington's Star
Windmill	Double Star	Fancy Star	Cross and Crown
Ohio Star	Pinwheel Quarto	Dutchman's Puzzle	Broken Dishes

Fig 60. Here's where to position each block on the quilt

Quilt detail. This corner of the quilt shows the sawtooth sashing and borders with a final frame of broad binding in blue

Assembling the blocks and units

1 Arrange the blocks in 4 vertical columns, using a design wall if possible. You will need 6 saw-tooth squares (half-square triangle units) to stitch between 2 blocks. Stitch 6 of the saw-tooth squares together in a line, keeping the seam orientation and the position of the dark and light fabrics consistent. If the sashing strip is a bit too long for the block, simply trim it to the same length as the edge to which it will be stitched, as shown in Fig 61. If you feel this looks unbalanced, repositioned the shortened triangle unit in the centre of a row by unpicking 3 of the saw-tooth squares and stitching them to the other side, as shown in Fig 62.

2 Stitch a set of 6 saw-tooth units between the blocks in each column.

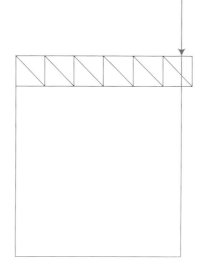

Fig 61. Trim the sashing strip to fit the block

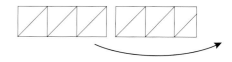

Fig 62. If desired, relocate the trimmed saw-tooth unit in the centre of the row

3 Now make three long strips of saw-tooth units to join the columns, including some smaller units as you work for unity and to ensure a good fit. Stitch these strips to the blocks to complete the central panel, as shown in Fig 63.

4 Now add sashing strips of saw-tooth units to the top, bottom and sides all around the outer edges of the panel in the same way as before.

5 Frame this panel with a border cut from 1½in (3.75cm) strips in a dark fabric. This can be pieced from different fabrics as in the quilt illustrated, or cut from a single fabric, if preferred.

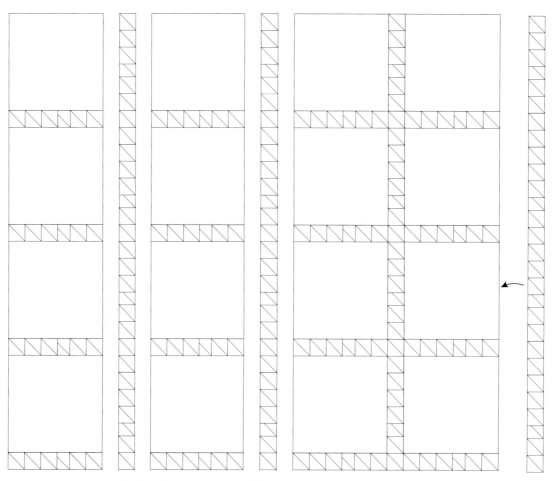

Fig 63. Joining the columns of blocks with the sashing strips

Making the outer saw-tooth border

The units for the outer saw-tooth border are slightly larger than those of the sashing strips. Cut the squares for these 3in (7.75cm). Make and join enough units to go all round the quilt.

Quilting the layers

1 Cut the wadding and the backing fabric so that they are 2–3in (5–7.5cm) larger all round than the quilt top to accommodate broad binding. Assemble the 3 layers of the quilt with the quilt top centred on the wadding, and the backing fabric underneath. Pin and then tack (baste) horizontal and vertical grid lines about 4in (10cm) apart across the entire quilt.

2 Quilt as desired by hand or machine (see page 116) using an appropriate quilting thread. Here the quilting follows the patchwork patterns of the blocks and sashing with contour quilting, and where there are larger areas these are filled with zigzags and geometrics. This was done in an improvisational way with no marking or measuring, with the feed dogs on the machine set to normal stitching (not free-motion) and a regular size stitch. If you can set your machine so that the needle is in the down position when stopping and turning the quilt, this will make the quilting easier. The thread used was variegated machine quilting thread.

Binding and finishing

1 Cut 4 binding strips 8 x 61in (20.25 x 155cm), piecing them together to make up the required lengths.

2 Trim the wadding and the backing fabric so that they project 1½in (4cm) beyond the quilt top.

3 Press the binding in half lengthways with wrong sides facing and attach it to the quilt following the instructions for broad binding with stitched mitres on page 119.

4 Don't forget to add a label to the back of the quilt stating who made it and when plus any other information desired.

Quilt detail. Using thread in a variegated colour avoids a harsh line and the stitching will blend with many of the colours in the quilt top

Cropped Pinwheels

In a marriage of opposites, this quilt combines light and dark, symmetry and A-symmetry for a look that's impossibly complicated. However, once you discover the technique you'll find the design really quite simple and not beyond your reach.

Based on traditional pinwheel blocks made from half-square triangle units, each block is trimmed differently so that no two are the same. They are set into light and dark blocks that can then be arranged to create further patterns. An alternative block layout was used for the quilt on page 84 and some further options are shown on page 85.

Cropped Pinwheels, 24 x 24in (61 x 61cm)
Quilted by the author

Fabric Notes...

One of the advantages to making scrap quilts that rely on a dark/light division in the values of the fabrics is th it doesn't matter if you run out of any one fabric. Just choose something from the appropriate set of dark or li and continue. In this quilt the contrast is very visible, which makes for a graphic interpretation of the design. Notice how the bright pink, orange and yellow in the pinwheels are echoed in the light stripes, where there are more pastel versions of these colours. The dark stripes contain a mixture of colours – green, blue and burgun – but the dark and light values are more important than the colours in the overall design. See also the alternat version of this quilt on page 84.

Cropped Pinwheels. Blocks are set together to create a strong diagonal design. If these were half-square triangle units, this layout would be known as Straight Furrows. This makes an eye-catching wall hanging

Tip

Scaling up
If you plan to make a bigger quilt scale up the pinwheel by cutting the squares 3½in (9cm) and cut the template larger. The seam allowance is included in the template so allow 1in (2.5cm) extra to the desired finished size.

Cropped Pinwheels

Finished block
5½ x 5½in (14 x 14cm)
Finished quilt
24 x 24in (61 x 61cm)

Assembly

Each block is like a half-square triangle unit with a diagonal split, having dark fabrics in one triangle and light fabrics in the other. The cropped pinwheels are set into these dark and light triangles. Make the pinwheels first then add the fabrics around them. You will need 16 light and 16 dark triangle units.

Making the dark triangles

1 Select 2 fabrics for the pinwheel with a high contrast – bright and dark work especially well together.

Fig 1. Stitch your squares together to make 4 half-square triangle units

2 Cut 2 squares 2½in (6.25cm) from each of these 2 fabrics. Place these right sides together in 2 pairs of 1 bright and 1 dark square and follow the instructions for making half-square triangle units on page 113. This makes 4 units like the ones shown in Fig 1.

Fig 2. Join the half-square triangle units to make the pinwheel

3 Stitch these units together in pairs and then stitch the pairs together to make the pinwheel, taking care to keep the orientation of the seams as shown Fig 2.

Fig 3. Trim the pinwheel on at least 2 sides, maintaining a four-sided shape

4 Place the pinwheel on the cutting board and trim off wedge-shaped pieces from at least 2 of the sides, keeping the pinwheel four sided. Don't cut off a corner, as this will create a fifth edge. For the first cropped pinwheel retain one of the right angles in a corner, as shown in Fig 3.

5 Cut a 6½in (16.5cm) square of tracing paper and then cut this across 1 diagonal to make a template for the triangle units.

6 Choose dark fabrics and stitch these to the pinwheel so there is sufficient fabric for the piece to be covered by the template, as shown in Fig 4. Try to maintain the straight grain of the fabrics on the 2 shorter sides of the triangle.

Fig 4. Add dark fabrics to the pinwheel to make a piece large enough to be covered by the triangle template

7 Pin the template to the pieced unit and cut round the paper carefully, using a ruler and rotary cutter on a cutting mat. Flat-headed Japanese flower pins are useful here because they allow the ruler to lie flat on top. The result is a neat triangle (Fig 5).

Fig 5. Trim the fabric using the template as a guide

Making the light triangles

1 Make the pinwheel first as in steps 1–3 on page 81, choosing a light/bright or light/dark combination of fabrics.

2 Crop the pinwheel in a different way. For example, cut from opposite sides to make a narrow shape. Refer to the photograph on page 80 for variations in cropping the pinwheels.

3 Set the pinwheel into light fabrics. You can alter the position of the pinwheel within the triangle. In the example in Fig 6 the pinwheel lies along the long edge of the triangle instead of fitting into the right angle as before.

4 Trim the block to the size of the paper template as before (see page 81).

Fig 7. Join a light triangle unit to a dark triangle unit to complete one block

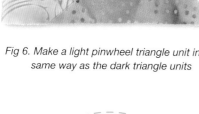

Fig 6. Make a light pinwheel triangle unit in the same way as the dark triangle units

Tip
Use the brights
The cropped pinwheels can be a showcase for the brightest fabrics in your collection. So dig out some of those pieces you thought you might never find a place for.

Making and joining the blocks

1 Place the light and dark triangles right sides together and stitch along the long side. Give the block a good steam press and trim off the extensions to the seam allowances to reduce bulk.

2 Make 16 blocks, varying the way you cut the pinwheels and their positions within the blocks to create movement in the quilt.

3 Arrange the blocks, using a design wall if possible, and referring to the photographs on pages 80 and 84 or creating your own arrangement. These blocks can be made into any number of different layouts. Some further options are shown on page 85.

4 Stitch the blocks together.

Quilting the layers

1 Cut the wadding and the backing fabric so that they are 1½in (4cm) larger all round than the quilt top. Assemble the 3 layers of the quilt with the quilt top centred on the wadding, and the backing fabric underneath. Pin and then tack (baste) horizontal and vertical grid lines about 4in (10cm) apart across the entire quilt.

2 Quilt as desired by hand or machine (see page 116) using an appropriate quilting thread. Alternatively, enlist the services of a quilter with a long-arm quilting machine (see page 116). I machine quilted with variegated machine quilting thread and a walking foot on the machine. I outlined the pinwheels and patches and filled in any larger spaces with freely stitched short lines such as zigzags and triangles.

Binding and finishing

1 Cut binding strips 4½in (11.5cm) wide, piecing them together as necessary to make up the required length.

2 Trim the backing and wadding to extend ¾in (2cm) beyond the edges of the quilt top.

3 Press the binding in half lengthways with wrong sides facing and attach it to the quilt following the instructions for straight binding with square corners on page 118.

4 Don't forget to add a label to the back of the quilt stating who made it and when plus any other information desired.

Quilt detail. As far as possible, plan to quilt in a continuous line, without too many stops and starts. If you have to move across the quilt, finish a line by doing several stitches on the spot, then clip the thread close to the surface

Cropped Pinwheels II. This variation uses mainly batik fabrics, where the tonal contrast is less pronounced than in the other version, giving a more delicate effect. Notice how I have arranged the blocks in a different layout too – Hopscotch

Alternative Block Layouts

Here are a few possible layouts for your pinwheel blocks. You can arrange them in many other ways too – just think of them as half-square triangle blocks.

Straight Furrows

Hopscotch

Barn Raising

Betsy's Star

Dutchman's Choice

Chevrons

Rooftops

Diamonds

Broken Cross

Streak o' Lightening

Mary's Puzzle

Triangles

Stars, Pinwheels & Colour Blocks

Stars and pinwheels dance across this quilt, interspersed with crazy Log Cabin style colour blocks in a riot of colour and life. Though it looks complicated and intricate, this quilt is surprisingly straightforward to make and will introduce you to some clever cutting and piecing techniques. As with all the quilts in this book, this is a wonderful opportunity to use up even your smallest fabric scraps and a great excuse – if ever one was needed – to buy plenty more.

Each block is made in a different way, making this a fantastic learning exercise and ensuring that you won't get bored partway through. It also provides a wide scope for individual interpretation through your colour choices, the cutting positions on the stars and colour blocks and the final arrangement of blocks. I have positioned the star and pinwheel blocks to form a dynamic diagonal band across the quilt, sweeping from the top right to the bottom left, but ultimately the positioning of the blocks is up to you.

Stars, Pinwheels and Colour Blocks, 58½ x 58½in (148.5 x 148.5cm)
Quilted by Beryl Cadman of Custom Quilting

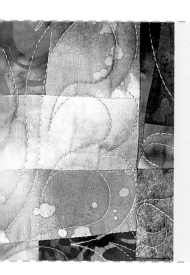

Fabric Notes...

Hand-dyed fabrics are popular with quilters; the appeal of transforming white fabric into a range of rainbow colours has sparked a wave of workshops and classes. Ingenious quilt tutors have developed ways of doing this without the need for a range of specialist equipment. Having tried my hand I had a collection of these hand-dyed fabrics, many of which were used in this quilt. After experimenting with my own hand dyes I decided that, rather than spending time rinsing and ironing, I would prefer to be sewing, so I now buy the (often more attractive) products of other more competent dyers.
Hand dyes combine well with textured fabrics and batiks. I teamed bright colours (yellow, pink and orange) with dark fabrics for contrast on the pinwheel and star blocks, so that they show up vividly against the background of colour blocks made in medium-value fabrics.

Stars, Pinwheels and Colour Blocks. I resisted the temptation to start sewing the blocks together before they were all made, then used a vertical design wall to arrange them to my satisfaction before completing the final construction of the quilt top

Stars, Pinwheels & Colour Blocks

Finished block
6½ x 6½in (16.5 x 16.5cm)
Finished quilt
58½ x 58½in (148.5 x 148.5cm)

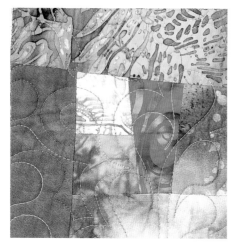

Sample block. There are many potential cutting patterns

Making the colour blocks

These are based on a crazy Log Cabin pattern with some variations. You will need 60 blocks in total but they can be assembled 8 at a time for ease and speed.

1 To make 8 blocks first cut 8 squares 9in (23cm) in harmonizing fabrics. Stack the fabrics together right sides up and press. Place them on the cutting mat and, referring to Fig 1, cut into 6 pieces through all layers using a ruler and rotary cutter. Cut freely and, as you do so, try to visualize the pieces in their finished size without the seam allowance. It may help to turn the cutting board a quarter turn with each cut. Move the sets of pieces slightly away from each other but keep them grouped in the cutting order until you come to stitch them together.

2 Pick up one set of a central piece, 5, and spread out on a flat surface. Now pick up the other centre pieces, 6. Team each piece 6 with a piece 5 in a different fabric. Place the triangles right sides together and stitch, taking a scant ¼in (7mm) seam allowance. Press the seams to one side. You now have 8 sets, as shown in Fig 2.

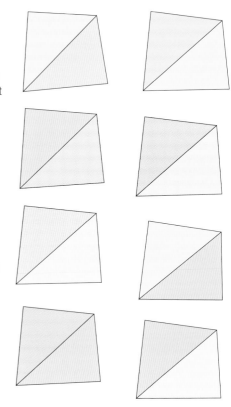

Fig 2. Making the centres

3 Now you need to add the strips around each stitched centre, mixing the fabrics as you work. Start with piece 4, making sure that you stitch it to the correct side of the centre, as shown in Fig 3.

Fig 1. Cutting the colour blocks

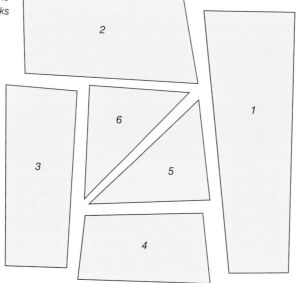

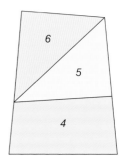

Fig 3. Adding the first strip

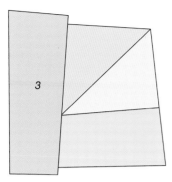

Fig 4. Adding the second strip

4 Next attach piece 3 (Fig 4). The strip will be a little longer than the centre and the next strip a little longer still. This does not matter as the pieces can be trimmed as you go and the blocks are squared up when they are finished.

5 Attach piece 2, as shown in Fig 5. Trim off the excess fabric after stitching.

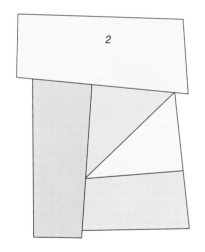

Fig 5. Adding the third strip

6 Finally attach piece 1, as shown in Fig 6. There are 6 pieces in each block, so working with 8 squares you can avoid colour repeats in any one block.

7 Cut a square of tracing paper 7in (17.75cm) and pin this to each of the blocks in turn using flat-ended Japanese

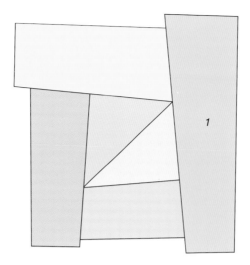

Fig 6. Adding the final strip

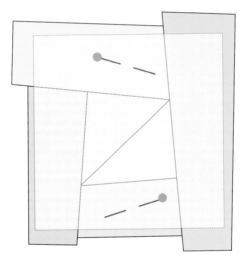

Fig 7. Trimming the colour blocks to size

flower pins, which will lie flat under your ruler, as shown in Fig 7. Cut round the template with a rotary cutter and ruler to square off the blocks.

8 Repeat the steps to make a total of 60 blocks. Each time you make a set of blocks you may like to vary the cutting pattern slightly to give each set a slightly different appearance. (See Fig 8, for some suggested cutting patterns.)

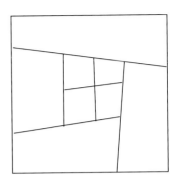

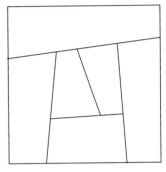

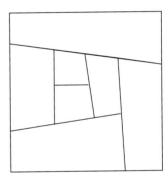

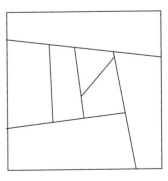

Fig 8. Alternative cutting patterns for the colour blocks

Making the tilted pinwheel blocks

You will need 3 fabrics for each pinwheel – 2 for the pinwheel and 1 for the corners. The pinwheel fabrics should be a high-contrast pair; either bright/dark or light/dark and the corner fabric should be in a different tone. You will need 12 pinwheel blocks in total.

1 From each of the pinwheel fabrics cut 1 square 3¾in (9.5cm).

2 Place the squares right sides together and, using the technique for making quarter-square triangles explained on page 113, make 4 bi-coloured triangles.

3 From the third fabric selected for the corners cut 2 squares 3⅜in (8.5cm) and divide these into 2 triangles by cutting across the diagonal. You now have 4 triangles altogether. Each of these will be stitched to a pieced triangle, as shown in Fig 9.

4 Stitch a pieced triangle to a corner triangle to make 4 squares, as shown in Fig 10, right.

5 To complete the pinwheel, stitch the resulting squares together, first into pairs then into the completed pinwheel (Fig 11).

6 Using short lengths of scrap fabric stitch a 1¾in (4.5cm) wide border to each side of the block in Log Cabin sequence. You can use one or more fabrics for this.

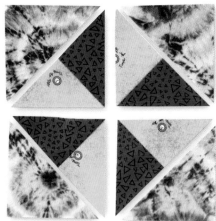

Fig 9. Preparing to join the corner triangles

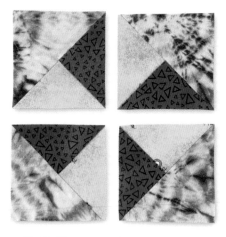

Fig 10. The corner triangles joined to the pieced triangles

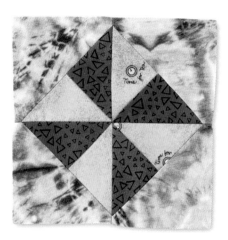

Fig 11. The completed pinwheel

7 Using the same size paper template as for the colour blocks (7in/17.75cm square), pin the template to the pinwheel at a skewed angle so that the corners of the paper touch the edges of the block (Fig 12). Cut around the paper to tilt the block using a ruler and rotary cutter.

Fig 12. Using the template to tilt the block

8 The paper template can be angled in two ways to tilt the pinwheel in opposite directions, as shown in Fig 13.

9 Make 12 tilted pinwheel blocks, tilting 6 in one direction and 6 in the other.

Fig 13. Pinwheels tilted in different directions

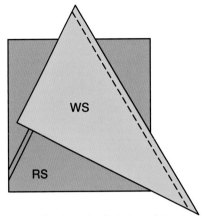

Fig 15. Mark the cutting lines

Fig 16. Stitch on the first star point

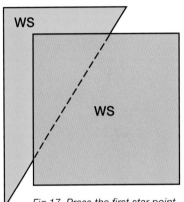

Fig 17. Press the first star point

Making the star blocks

If you look closely at the quilt you will see that there are 3 large straight star blocks and 5 smaller tilted ones. We will make the larger ones first. You will need a minimum of 2 fabrics for each star block – see the sample blocks in the Fabric Focus box overleaf. Choose bright fabrics for each star and a good contrast for the background squares.

1 From background fabric(s) cut 8 squares 2¾in (7cm). Select 4 of these and mark the star points with a fabric marker, as shown in Fig 14, below. Vary the shapes and sizes of the points – long and narrow, short and fat – with each square.

2 Take one of the squares and mark a second line for each star point a scant ¼in (7mm) away on the star side of each original marked line, as shown in Fig 15, above. The original line is the sewing line and the new line is the cutting line for the star. Do not cut out.

3 Cut a piece of star fabric that will adequately cover the first corner of the background fabric and place this right side down on top, positioning the raw edge along one cutting line, as shown in Fig 16. Stitch the 2 layers of fabric together a scant ¼in (7mm) from the edge, along the stitching line of the background piece.

Fig 18. Add the second star point

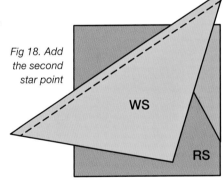

4 Flip the star fabric over to lie flat against the background; press. Place the square on your cutting mat, wrong side uppermost, as shown in Fig 17. Using the background square as a guide cut away the excess star fabric from around the edge. Now trim the background fabric away from behind the star point along the cutting line you marked in step 2.

5 Cut another piece of star fabric for the second point and, using the cutting line as a guide, place it in position. Stitch the seam as before, as shown in Fig 18.

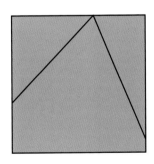

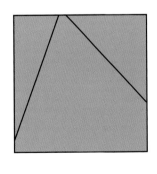

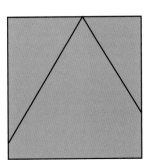

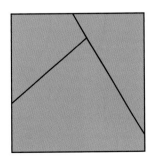

Fig 14. Mark the star points on the background squares

6 Press the second star point over, as shown in Fig 19. Place it on the cutting mat wrong sides uppermost and trim around the background square. Cut away the background fabric from behind the star point, as before.

7 Press the square. It should look something like the square in Fig 20. Repeat this procedure with the other 3 background squares to make 4 star-point units altogether.

8 Cut 1 square 2¾in (7cm) for the centre of the block in star fabric or another fabric of your choice.

9 Arrange the squares into the block sequence on a flat surface and stitch the squares together as indicated by the arrows on Fig 21.

10 Check the size of the block and, if necessary, trim slightly to match the size of the colour blocks.

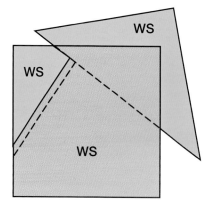

Fig 19. Press the second star point

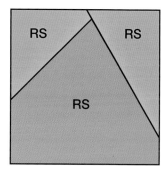

Fig 20. The star-point unit

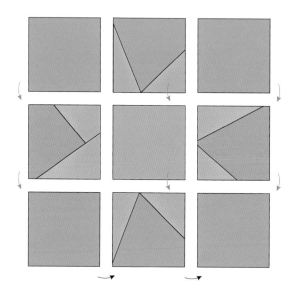

Fig 21. Assembling the units to make the block

Fabric Focus

This block uses just two highly contrasting fabrics, one for the star and one for the background. This arrangement will make the star blocks very prominent in the quilt.

In this block a number of different toning prints combine in the background and two fabrics create the star: one for the points and one for the centre. Notice how this block has a subtler appearance than the other block, which uses just two fabrics.

Making the tilted star blocks

Some of the star blocks in the quilt have been tilted in the same way as the pinwheels (see page 90). These blocks are made smaller by cutting the background squares 2¼in (5.7cm).

1 Follow steps 1–9 for the star blocks, on pages 91–92, to make a smaller star block using 2¼in (5.7cm) squares.

2 Using short lengths of scrap fabric, stitch a 1¾in (4.5cm) wide border to each side of the block in Log Cabin sequence. You can use one or more fabrics for this.

3 Using the same size paper template as for the colour blocks – 7in (17.75cm) square – pin the template to the block at a skewed angle so that the corners of the paper touch the edges of the block. Cut around the paper to create a skewed block, as before, so that they resemble Fig 22, right. Make 8 star blocks altogether, some straight, some skewed.

Joining the blocks

When you have made the 81 blocks organize them in a large square of 9 x 9 blocks, using a design wall, if possible. Use the picture on page 87 as a guide or create your own arrangement. Stitch the blocks together in rows then join the rows to finish.

Quilting the layers

1 Cut the wadding and the backing fabric so that they are 1½in (4cm) larger all round than the quilt top. Assemble the 3 layers of the quilt with the quilt top centred on the wadding, and the backing fabric underneath. Pin and then tack (baste) horizontal and vertical grid lines about 4in (10cm) apart across the entire quilt.

2 Quilt as desired by hand or machine (see page 116) using an appropriate quilting thread. Alternatively, enlist the services of a quilter with a long-arm quilting machine (see page 116).

Binding and finishing

1 Cut binding strips 2½in (6.25cm) wide, piecing them together as necessary to make up the required length.

2 Trim the wadding and backing fabrics a scant ¼in (0.75cm) beyond the edge of the quilt top.

3 Press the binding in half lengthways with wrong sides facing and attach it to the quilt following the instructions for straight binding with square corners on page 118.

4 Don't forget to add a label to the back of the quilt stating who made it and when plus any other information desired.

Fig 22. The tilted star block

Snail Trail

The Snail Trail block is a traditional design that relies on the correct placement of contrasting fabrics for its effect. Contrast between the dark and light areas is traditionally pronounced but I have deliberately used low contrast in some areas so that sometimes the blocks appear to be hidden and the viewer has to study the quilt to find them. If you choose to do the same, use a design wall so you can stand away from the blocks as you make them. When you are working close to them it is difficult to see the block pattern emerging.

Although all the seams are straight, an illusion of curves is created, making an intriguing puzzle. Using the technique of foundation piecing makes the construction of the blocks easier and ensures accuracy because they are only 4in (10.25cm) square.

Snail Trail, 24in x 24in (61 x 61cm)
Quilted by the author

Fabric Notes...

I selected two groups of fabrics with a fairly close contrast based on a blue palette with just a few indications of pink, which are carefully balanced across the composition, providing a relief from the mainly blue fabrics. Included are batik, floral, geometric and marble fabrics in a mixture of pattern scales.

Snail Trail. This is a design that relies for its effectiveness on contrast. Here I have made the contrast between the two values as medium and dark, which makes for a fairly muted interpretation

Snail Trail

Finished block
4 x 4in (10.25 x 10.25cm)

Finished quilt
24in x 24in (61 x 61cm)

Fabric requirements

Foundation material: ½ yard (0.5 metre) of Stitch 'n' Tear

Markers: fine line felt-tip pen, sharp pencil and ruler

Cotton fabric: a total of 2–3¼ yards (2–3 metres) of scraps ranging over the blue palette in contrasting values of light and dark. The biggest pieces needed for the blocks are 3½in (9cm) squares

Binding: ½ yard (0.5 metre) of cotton fabric

Backing: cotton fabric(s) made up to 32 x 32in (81 x 81cm)

Wadding: 32 x 32in (81 x 81cm)

Assembly

The blocks are assembled using foundation piecing. This involves using a template for each block that is traditionally marked on paper or fine fabric to create the foundation. Foundations can be permanent (left in the quilt) in which case they are made of something like muslin, or temporary in which case they are removed after stitching. Either way the quilting fabric is pinned to the foundation and stitched using the guidelines to ensure accuracy every time. I have found that Stitch 'n' Tear makes an excellent foundation because it can be easily torn away after stitching.

Making the four-patch centre unit

1 Make the centre four patch by cutting strips 1¼ x 3in (3.25 x 7.5cm), 1 from the dark set and 1 from the light set of fabrics.

2 Stitch these together in pairs of 1 light and 1 dark strip along the long edge. Press the seams to the darker side.

3 Now cross cut two 1¼in (3.25cm) sections from the joined strips as shown in Fig 1, above right.

4 Reverse 1 of the sections and stitch these right sides together, locking the centre seam to match the point as indicated in Fig 2. Press this seam open. You have completed the four-patch unit.

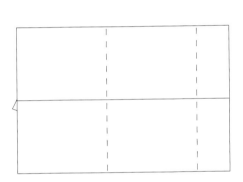

Fig 1. Cut two 1¼in (3.25cm) sections from your joined light and dark strips

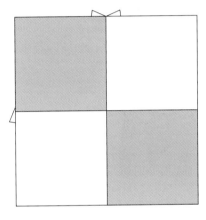

Fig 2. Reverse 1 strip section and stitch to the first section to make the central four-patch unit

A subtle dark binding gives a neat, discreet finish to this quilt

Foundation piecing

1 Cut the 'Stitch 'n' Tear into 25 squares 6in (15.25cm).

2 Tape each of these squares over the template in Fig 3 and trace the design with a fine black pen, including the outer dotted line. There is no need to put the numbers and letters on the tracing because you can use the diagram for the placement of the dark and light fabrics.

3 On the back of one of the traced foundation squares use a sharp pencil to extend the crossed centre lines to the outer corners. This will help to position the centre four-patch unit accurately.

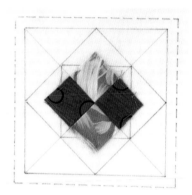

Fig 4. Pin the four-patch unit to the tracing, aligning diagonals

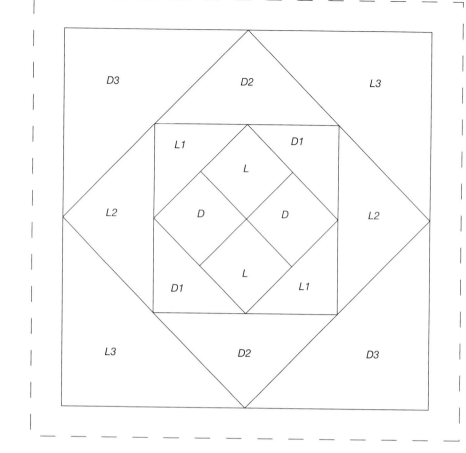

Fig 3. Snail Trail template

4 Pin the four-patch unit to the foundation on the reverse side to the traced design, lining up the centre point and the seams with the extended centre lines and making sure that the dark and light fabrics are correctly positioned as in Fig 4. Secure with pins or tacking.

5 Cut two dark triangles that will adequately cover areas D1. Pin one of these right side down over the centre four patch, aligning raw edges. You may have to hold it up to the light to ensure that it covers the correct area.

6 Now turn the foundation square over and stitch along the drawn line joining D1 to the four-patch unit and stitching through the foundation. Make a couple of extra stitches to ensure seams won't come undone when the Stitch 'n' Tear is removed.

7 Trim the seam down to a scant ¼in (0.75cm) taking care not to cut through the foundation. Flip the dark triangle over flat against the foundation and press. Repeat with the opposite dark triangle (Fig 5).

8 Now cut 2 light triangles for L1 and repeat, as shown in Fig 6.

Fig 5. Attaching the first triangles

9 Repeat the process for the second round, placing dark triangles first, then the light ones, stitching on the appropriate lines, trimming seams and pressing patches flat to the foundation. Your piece should now look like the one in Fig 7.

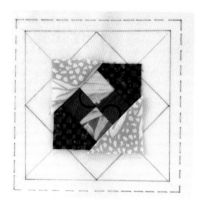

Fig 6. Attaching the second pair of triangles to complete the first 'round'

Fig 7. Second 'round' completed

10 For the final round cut the triangles large enough to extend over the dotted line. This will provide the seam allowance to join the blocks together. Stitch the triangles in place.

Fig 8. The finished block

11 Press the block and place it face down on the cutting board. Trim away excess fabric through all layers on the dotted lines. Your finished block should look like the one in Fig 8, with seam allowances all round.

12 Repeat to make a total of 25 blocks.

In this scaled-down version of the Snail Trail quilt there are 16 blocks 3in (7.5cm) set 4 across by 4 down with a borders of strips. Note the wider range of colours and in particular the use of yellow and orange for some of the tiny centre squares. The quilting was done with a variegated thread

Joining the blocks

1 Refer to the picture on page 96 as a guide and stitch the blocks together 5 across by 5 down, matching points where appropriate. Press seams open as you work. Remove the foundation (Stitch 'n' Tear) carefully. I find it helps to use a ruler and the point of a seam ripper to score along the stitching lines, making it possible to lift away the foundation in complete pieces rather than shredding it.

Adding the border

The border is composed of the largest triangles set in a chevron around the outer edges with the values of the fabrics arranged to complement the blocks.

1 From your scrap selection cut 44 squares 2⅞in (7.25cm). Sort these into contrasting pairs and make up half-square triangle units following the instructions on page 113.

2 For the top and bottom of the quilt sew together 2 strips of 10 units in a chevron pattern. Add these to the top and bottom of the quilt panel, matching seams. For the 2 opposite sides sew together 2 sets of 12 units and add these to the sides. Press the quilt.

Quilting the layers

1 Cut the wadding and the backing fabric so that they are 1½in (4cm) larger all round than the quilt top. Assemble the 3 layers of the quilt with the quilt top centred on the wadding, and the backing fabric underneath. Pin and then tack (baste) horizontal and vertical grid lines about 4in (10cm) apart across the entire quilt.

2 Using monofilament thread, quilt by machine in a grid of diagonal straight lines from edge to edge across the seams.

Binding and finishing

1 Cut binding strips 2½in (6.25cm) wide, piecing them together as necessary to make up the required length.

2 Trim the wadding and backing fabrics a scant ¼in (0.75cm) beyond the edge of the quilt top.

3 Press the binding in half lengthways with wrong sides facing and attach it to the quilt following the instructions for straight binding with square corners on page 118.

4 Don't forget to add a label to the back of the quilt stating who made it and when plus any other information desired.

Triptych Wall Hanging

Abandon the concept of blocks set in a formal grid to create your own small 'art' quilts by combining all the techniques you've learned from this book and more. I started to experiment in this way, first by using small, simple blocks made from squares, triangles and strips, then adding collaged sections to connect them and borders made with curved seams. The results of these experiments are illustrated in the Gallery (see page 110). Working on these small pieces gave me the idea for this three-part wall hanging, which incorporates a variety of techniques to create the combined pattern elements such as zigzags, diamonds and triangles, with more organic areas made by sewing randomly shaped fabric scraps together. This was exhibited at the 2005 Festival of Quilts, Birmingham UK in the 'Small Contemporary' section.

Triptych Wall Hanging, each section 36 x 7¼in (91.5 x 18.5cm)
Quilted by the author

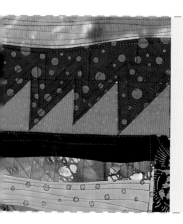

Fabric Notes...

Bold, bright colours with good contrast and large- and small-scale prints add interest and visual texture. I used the grey and black leaf batik in all three pieces, putting it in various positions to balance the weight of its large scale across the overall composition. Other unusual fabrics are the over-dyed African print and small pieces of Japanese indigo block print. These small quilts are ideal to showcase unusual fabrics, maybe the last scrap of a piece you have been saving for something special.

Triptych Wall Hanging.
These three panels can be
hung as a triptych or individually
depending on available space

Triptych Wall Hanging

Getting started

Begin by selecting 5-8 different fabrics that will harmonize – these can be added to as you progress. Quite small pieces can be used in the freely pieced collage sections. Don't be afraid to use some relatively big pieces if you include a larger scale pattern such as the grey and black leaf print in my hanging. As you work, try to balance the brighter colours such as orange, yellow and red across the quilt's surface to keep the eye moving around.

Making the Seminole squares

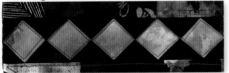

Fig 1. Seminole strip

1 Select 2 fabrics with a good contrast. From 1 of the fabrics cut a strip 9in x 1½in (23 x 3.75cm).

2 Cut 2 strips from the other fabric 9in x 1¾in (23 x 4.5cm). Stitch these together along the length with the narrower strip in the middle. Press the seams away from the centre strip. Make sure the end of the strip section is trimmed at 90 degrees and then cut 5 sections 1½in (3.75cm) from the strip, as shown in Fig 2.

3 Place the sections together, stepping them so that the points of the centre squares match to form a row of diamonds.

4 Cut a 3½in (9cm) square of the same fabric as used for the outer strips and divide this into 2 triangles by cutting across 1 diagonal. Add 1 to each end of your row, as in Fig 3. Stitch the strips and triangles together then press the seams open.

5 Trim away the stepped edge to ¼in (0.75cm) beyond the points of the diamonds, as shown by the chalk lines in Fig 4. Trim the short ends to create the desired width.

Fabric requirements

Cotton fabric: a large selection of fabrics - take the opportunity to use some of your most treasured scraps
Backing: cotton fabric(s) made up to three pieces 40 x 11¼in (101.5 x 28.5cm)
Wadding: three pieces 40 x 11¼in (101.5 x 28.5cm)

Fig 2. Cutting the joined strips into sections

Fig 3. Arranging the sections to form the diamond pattern

Fig 4. Trimming the strip to size

Prairie points are small inserts that are trapped in the seams. Use them to balance a bright colour across the composition when you have no room for another patch

The template diagram on the left shows numbered equilateral triangles from bottom to top: 1, 2, 3, 4, 5, 6, 7, 8, 9, 10, 11, 12, 13.

Fig 6. Triangle template

Making the strip of equilateral triangles

Fig 5. Triangle strip

This strip (Fig 5) was made using foundation piecing, a foolproof way of getting accuracy with small or awkward shapes that would be difficult to piece in the regular way.

1 To make the template for marking out the foundations (Fig 6), I drew the equilateral triangles on isometric graph paper. This is marked in a grid of triangles and whatever size you want can be highlighted with a fine pen. Use this paper to mark the size of triangles and the length required. Add a dotted line ¼in (0.75cm) around the outer edges for the seam allowance as in Fig 7.

Fig 7. Use isometric paper to draw your template or trace the template provided

2 Using Stitch 'n' Tear for the foundation, cut a strip that will adequately cover the drawing, including the dotted lines, plus a bit extra. Secure the Stitch 'n' Tear' over the drawing with small pieces of masking tape and trace the drawing accurately, including the dotted line around the outer edges, as shown in Fig 8.

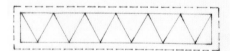

Fig 8. Transfer the template on to Stitch 'n' Tear

3 Select 2 fabrics with a good contrast. The patches are placed on the blank side of the foundation and the stitching is done on the other side along the lines.

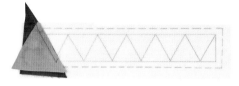

Fig 9. Stitch the first 2 triangles together through the foundation

4 Begin at one end of the strip and cut a triangle of one of the fabrics that will adequately cover the end triangle marked 1. Place this right side up over shape 1 on the blank side of the foundation. You may have to hold it up to the light to ensure that it covers the end triangle and goes over the dotted line. Now cut a triangle of the second fabric, which will adequately cover triangle number 2. Place this right side down against the first triangle then turn the foundation over and stitch along the line between shapes marked 1 and 2 (Fig 9). Turn back and trim away the seam allowance to ¼in (0.75cm) beyond the stitching line.

Fig 10. Press the first seam

5 Flip the second triangle over so that it lies flat against the foundation as shown in Fig 10 and press.

Fig 11. Continue in the same way

6 Continue adding triangles in the same way, alternating the colours along the strip, as shown in Fig 11.

Fig 12. Trim the strip around the dotted lines on the foundation to finish

7 At this stage the edges will look quite untidy, but don't worry about this; as long as all the triangles extend beyond the dotted line it will be fine when the strip has been trimmed. When you have covered all the triangles place the strip on the cutting board with the foundation showing uppermost and trim along the dotted line around the edges. This will leave a neat strip, as shown in Fig 12. Leave the Stitch 'n' Tear in place until the strip has been stitched into the quilt to help stabilize the bias edges. When you are ready to remove it, score along the stitching lines with the point of a seam ripper and the paper can be lifted away from the back.

Making the half-square triangle strip

Fig 13. Half-square triangle strip

This is an adaptation of the quick-pieced half-square triangles on page 113, which can be used on smaller units.
1 Select 2 fabrics and cut 2½in (6.25cm) strips of each one, 10in (25.5cm) or longer depending on how many triangle units are required for your hanging.

Fig 14. Stitch ¼in (0.75cm) each side of the diagonal lines

2 Place the strips right sides together in pairs. Mark off 2½in (6.25cm) squares and then draw a zigzag line across the diagonals. Stitch ¼in (0.75cm) both sides of the diagonal lines, as shown in Fig 14.

3 Cut the squares apart and then cut along the diagonal lines. Press the seams to the darker side and trim off the seam allowances where they project. You now have some half-square triangles as shown in Fig 15.

4 Stitch the triangle units in a line to the desired length.

Fig 15. Cut the squares apart then cut along the diagonal lines to create the squares

Stitching curved seams without templates
1 Cut 2 strips of fabric about 3in (7.5cm) wide and slightly longer than the piece you are planning to stitch it to.

2 Place these on the cutting board right sides uppermost and overlapping each other by approximately 1½in (4cm).

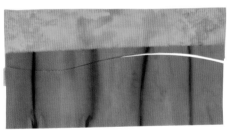

Fig 16. Cut the two fabrics at once in a gentle curve

3 Cut through both layers, introducing gentle curves as you cut, as shown in Fig 16.

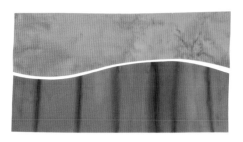

Fig 17. Remove the unwanted sections

4 Discard the narrow edges to the side of each strip (one will be on the top and the other with be underneath). You will now have 2 pieces of fabric that fit snugly together with curved edges like the ones shown in Fig 17.

Fig 18. Ease the edges together and pin the seam

5 Flip one of the strips over so that they are right sides together (at this point it will seem as if they won't fit) and ease the raw edges together, pinning down the length of the strips with the pins at right angles to the edges as in Fig 18.

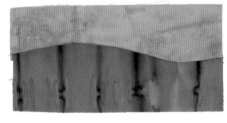

Fig 19. Stitch the seam, taking a scant seam allowance, then press neatly

6 Stitch, taking a scant seam allowance. Press the seam over to one side, then press on the right side (Fig 19).

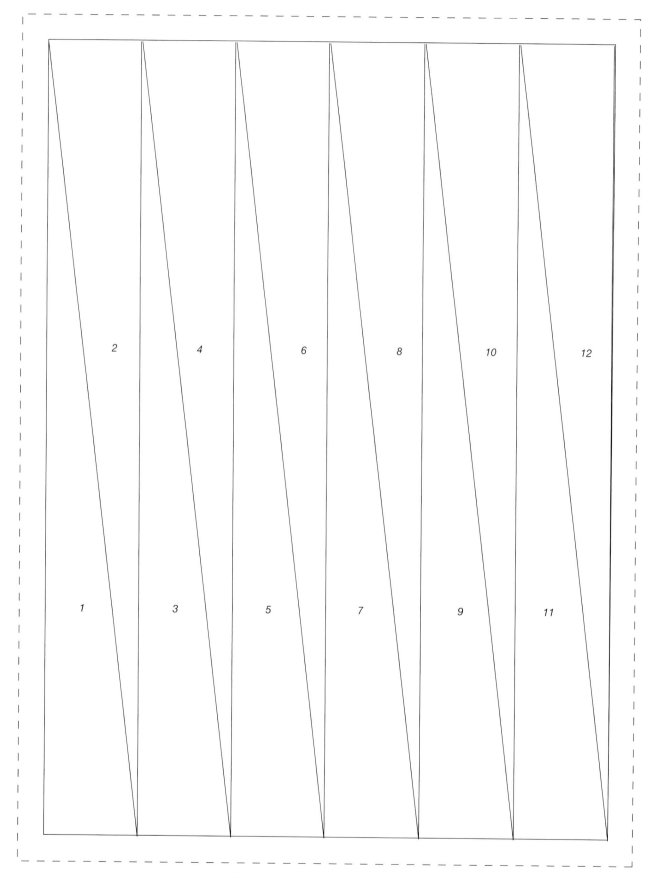

Fig 21. Zigzag panel template

Making the zigzag panel

Fig 20. Zigzag panel

The zigzag panel (Fig 20) is also foundation pieced. Trace the template in Fig 21 and use the technique of foundation piecing, following the numbers in the same way as for the equilateral triangle strip.

Stitching quartered rectangles

1 Select 2 fabrics and cut one 3½ x 5½in (9 x 14cm) rectangle from each one. Place them right sides together on the cutting board and cut across both diagonals, as shown in Fig 22.

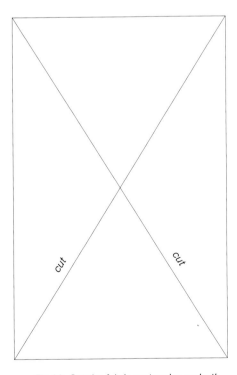

Fig 22. Cut the fabric rectangles on both diagonals as indicated here

Fig 23. Join pairs of triangles into larger triangles

2 Rearrange the resulting triangles to make 2 bi-coloured rectangles and stitch pairs of triangles, as shown in Fig 23.

3 Place the pieced triangles right sides together and stitch across the diagonal, matching the centre point. This will yield two quartered rectangles.

Fig 24. Stitch 2 pieced triangles together to complete each rectangle

Making prairie points

Fig 25. Prairie points are caught in the seams

These small folded triangles (Fig 25) can be trapped in a seam to provide a focus of colour and a three dimensional detail.

1 Cut a square of fabric 2½in (6.25cm) or larger depending on the scale you are working on. Fold in half across the diagonal and press. Fold in half again. All the raw edges are now on the longest side of the triangle (Fig 26).

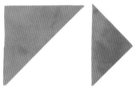

Fig 26. Fold a square diagonally and fold it again to make the prairie point

2 Pin the folded triangles in position and when the seam is stitched they will be caught in the seam.

Adding the 'collage' elements

The collage elements are made by stitching together random pieces of fabric – small squares, rectangles strips and triangles. It is not possible to give an exact pattern for these but here are some guidelines:

• When cutting shapes, make them asymmetrical, measuring by eye rather than trying to be too exact. Cutting these with scissors rather than a rotary cutting set might help.

• Try making a four-patch unit then add Log Cabin style strips all round, or sew 3 or more strips together of unequal widths, some with straight seams and some with curved seams.

• Include some triangles or small motifs from printed fabric.

Assembling the quilt

1 To combine all the elements made with these techniques use a design wall to arrange the more structured parts – such as the triangle and diamond strips – with the collaged pieces. Join sections with both straight and curved seams. Try to arrange the composition using different-sized pieces of fabric with a variety of scales in the prints and pay attention to the balance of colours, particularly the brighter, more eye-catching ones. During workshops, some students have difficulty making decisions when it comes to the final composition of a piece, but often it is the quickly made, more spontaneous pieces that are most successful. The simplest solution to a design problem is often the most effective one, so just trust your instincts and go for it!

2 When you are satisfied with the result complete the final stitching and remove the Stitch 'n' Tear in the foundation-pieced sections. Press the quilt top.

Finishing the outer edges

Small quilts like this can be finished without binding the edges, here's how.

1 Make up a piece of backing consisting of 2 pieces of fabric with a seam across the middle, as shown in the stitching diagram, Fig 27. Leave a gap in the seam – this is where you will turn the quilt through.

2 Place the quilt top and backing right sides together. Press, pin, then trim the outer edges of both quilt top and backing to make them the same size, with the wrong side of the quilt uppermost. It is at this stage that the edges can be shaped, like the points at the base of the triptych quilts or the wavy edges of the quilts in the Gallery (see pages 110–111).

3 Cut a piece of wadding slightly larger than the quilt, place this on a flat surface, then place the quilt wrong side down on top of the wadding with the backing right side down on top. Pin through all layers.

4 Using a walking foot on your machine, if possible, stitch all round the outer edges with the backing on top and the wadding underneath. If you do not have a walking foot it is advisable to tack the three layers together first.

5 Trim the wadding close to the stitching and clip corners across to reduce bulk.

6 Turn the quilt to the right side through the gap in the backing. Finger press the seam around the quilt so it lies along the outer edge, then close the gap in the backing with neat slipstitches. Your quilt is now ready for quilting by hand or machine.

Quilting the layers

Look for interesting machine quilting thread such as variegated colours with shiny or matt finishes. Quilting is done with the feed dogs engaged – regular stitching – but you could disengage the feed dogs and do some free-motion quilting if you prefer.

1 To gain confidence make up a dummy 'sandwich' of the wadding between 2 pieces of fabric about 8in (20cm) square and practise some designs on a little sampler. If you can, fix your machine so that when you stop stitching the needle stays down. This helps when changing direction and will keep the work anchored as you turn the quilt in the machine.

2 Using machine quilting thread, follow the patches by outlining them close to the seams and break up any larger shapes with zigzags, squares and triangles in short straight lines. Stitch wavy lines along the curved seams. Work from the centre of the quilt to the edge.

3 Don't forget to add a label to the back of the quilt stating who made it and when plus any other information desired.

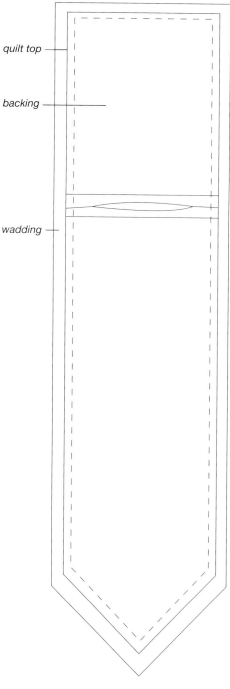

quilt top

backing

wadding

Fig 27. Stitching diagram. If you want to shape the quilt to a point, as shown, or to another shape, now is the time to do it

Tip

Big and beautiful
Don't be afraid to include some relatively large pieces of fabric in your final composition. Remember that the quilting will break up these bigger shapes and add surface texture.

Quilt detail. Be creative with your quilt stitches, sometimes echoing the shapes of the pieces, at other times balancing the angles with curves and the curves with straight lines. As far as possible work in a continuous line to avoid too many stops and starts. Stitching over the same line twice occasionally is often more convenient than breaking the line and having to cut the thread.

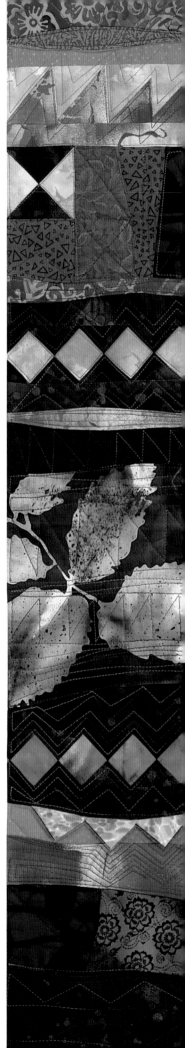

Gallery

Making a small-scale art quilt is an excellent way to experiment with techniques you haven't tried before or perhaps wouldn't like to attempt on a larger scale. Take the opportunity to put together daring colour combinations and experiment with stitching curved seams and other freeform techniques. Here are the small-scale art quilts that inspired the wall hanging on page 101.

Simple blocks combined with collage elements make up the centre panel of this mini quilt. The dark border in two fabrics has a pinwheel as a corner feature, balancing the pink striped fabric. Bold quilting and buttons complete this striking composition.

This quilt was made to give a showcase to the small printed panels from South Africa. Bugle beads and two novelty buttons were added for a whimsical touch.

Asymmetrical Log Cabin blocks were the starting point for these two quilts. The blocks have been extended with saw-tooth sashing strips and borders pieced with curved seams.

Four simple blocks set together with green sashing are extended with saw-tooth edges on two sides and prairie points on the other sides. Dark borders form a frame and a corner detail of half-square triangle units balances the saw-tooth section further in.

Techniques

Patchwork and quilting are such a diverse field and cover so many different processes that to document them all would fill a whole book. Here I am concerned with useful techniques that are relevant to the quilts in this book. For the beginner there are numerous books that cover all the basic techniques with advice on which equipment is most useful and how to choose fabrics to begin your collection or stash.

Wherever possible, I try to use rotary cutting and quick-piecing techniques and avoid templates unless absolutely necessary, although I will admit that when I first saw rotary cutters I wrote them off as a gadget that 'wouldn't catch on' – how wrong can you be! Now I am a firm advocate of all things that speed up the processes of construction.

Metric Conversion

If you are a mathematician you may be a little confused by the metric conversions as they are not exactly comparable. The metric rulers designed for quilters are marked out in 0.25 centimetre sections to avoid a confusing array of lines. This means that the imperial measurements have been multiplied by 2.54, then rounded up or down to the nearest quarter centimetre to comply with the rulers. When following the instructions, stick to either the imperial or metric measurements, do not try to combine the two systems. When beginning a new project it is always advisable to make a sample block.

Quick cutting

When faced with a basket of scrap fabrics that are all different shapes and sizes I have developed a method of cutting the pieces that involves first roughly cutting the size of square or other shape needed with a pair of scissors. When I have a good selection I begin to stack them up and cut them accurately with a rotary-cutting set. When I demonstrate this to students I can see them looking a bit sceptical at first but they soon agree with me that it is effective in speeding up the process, especially when you only need one or two squares from each fabric in the basket.

1 For each shape required (usually a square) make a paper template the required size. Just hold the paper over the fabric and cut round it – you don't have to be precise or even pin the paper to the fabric, it just ensures that the piece or fabric will be big enough. Make sure that the straight grain of the fabric runs parallel with the sides of the square or rectangle.

2 Stack up the squares in groups of 6 or 8, lining up one of the corners, steam press them together and cut out accurately on the cutting board. You can use the grid on the board or the ruler. I prefer to use the grid on the ruler for shapes less than 6in (15.25cm) as you can trap the fabrics underneath the ruler, ensuring that they will not move while you are cutting. It is very easy to make a mistake when rotary cutting. Even seasoned quilters like myself sometimes do this so remember the old saying 'measure twice, cut once' and check each time before you cut.

3 When 2 fabrics are required for a unit, for example in half- and quarter-square triangle units, take the opportunity to pair up the 2 fabrics and put them right sides together when you cut them out, thereby saving yourself a job later.

4 If cutting triangles from squares remember to cut across the diagonal line as well.

Tip
Light on top
When pairing fabrics ready for marking the diagonal lines, always put the paler one on top as it is easier to mark a light fabric. When marking use a fine line marker or pencil – thick lines will distort the accuracy of your piecing.

Adding seam allowances

The following measurements are based on sewing an accurate ¼in (0.75cm) seam.

To cut out a square simply add ½in (1.5cm) to the finished size. For example, cut a 3½in (9cm) square for a 3in (7.5cm) finished square or 4½in (11.75cm) for a 4in (10.25cm) finished square, and so on.

To cut a rectangle just add ½in (1.25cm) to the finished length and width of the finished size required.

For half-square triangle units, rather than cut the triangles out individually it is possible to construct them with squares, sew first and then cut (see right). The formula for how much extra to add to the square you cut for the finished size of the unit is to add ⅞in (2.25cm). For a 3in (7.5cm) finished square you would cut squares 3⅞in (9.75cm), for example.

Quarter-square triangle units can be made quickly from squares following the instructions opposite. The formula for how much extra to add to the squares you cut for the finished size of the unit is to add 1¼in (3cm). For a 3in (7.5cm) finished square you would cut squares 4¼in (10.5cm), for example.

For Flying Geese you will need 2 fabrics. You can make 4 units at once following the instructions on page 114, where you can find cutting sizes too.

A diamond in a square can be made using my quick-piecing technique, explained on page 115. Refer to the instructions there for cutting sizes.

Quick-piecing methods

Here are my methods for quick piecing, which not only speed up the process of making quilting units but also give accurate results. I have used these methods for most of the quilts in this book.

Making quick-pieced half-square triangle units

Fig 1. Half-triangle unit

1 Cut squares ⁷/₈in (2.25cm) larger than the finished size of the unit (the size it will be when stitched into the quilt).

2 Place 2 squares with different values (light and dark, for example) right sides together and draw a diagonal line on the lighter fabric. Stitch ¼in (0.75cm) away from the line on both sides as in Fig 2.

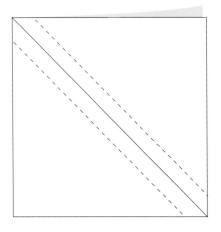

Fig 2. Pair the squares, place right sides together and stitch ¼in (0.75cm) either side of the diagonal

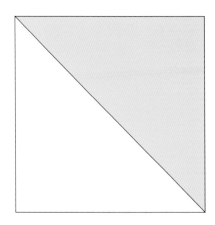

Fig 3. Cut along the diagonal to produce 2 bi-coloured half-triangle units

3 Cut down the drawn line and open out the fabrics (Fig 3). You now have 2 bi-coloured half-square triangle units. Press the seams neatly open or to one side.

Making quarter-square triangle units

1 Cut squares 1¼in (3cm) larger than the finished size of the unit (the size it will be when stitched into the quilt).

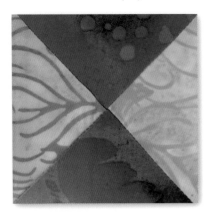

Fig 4. Quarter-square triangle unit

2 Place 2 squares with different values (light and dark, for example) right sides together and draw 2 diagonal lines. Stitch exactly as illustrated in Fig 5, ¼in (0.75cm) away from the marked lines.

3 Cut along both marked lines. This produces 4 bi-coloured triangles like the 2 shown in Fig 6. Place these right sides together in pairs and stitch along the long edge, maintaining the ¼in (0.75cm) seam allowance as usual.

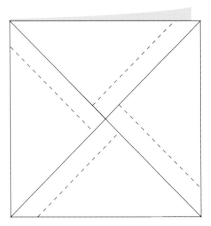

Fig 5. Pair the squares, place right sides together and stitch ¼in (0.75cm) from the diagonals exactly as shown here

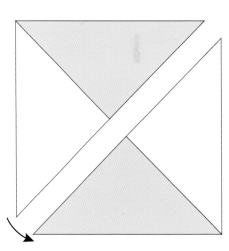

Fig 6. Cut along the diagonals to create four bi-coloured triangles. Join in pairs

4 Open out the fabrics and press the completed squares. Each square will be like the one in Fig 4.

Making quick-pieced Flying Geese

Fig 7. Flying Geese unit

This rectangular unit can be used for borders or to create the points on a star as for the Eight-Pointed Star used in the Galaxy of Stars and Scraps quilt, page 39.

1 Cut the fabric for the large triangle in a square that is the finished width of the unit plus 1¼in (3cm). Cut the fabric for the smaller triangles into 4 squares the finished height of the unit plus ⁷⁄₈in (2.25cm).

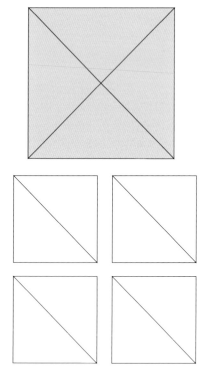

Fig 8. Draw diagonal lines on the squares as shown

2 Draw 2 diagonal lines on the right side of the large square. Draw 1 diagonal line on the wrong side of each small square as shown in Fig 8.

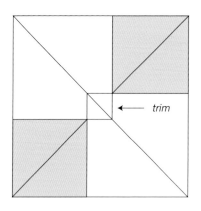

Fig 9. Position the smaller squares on the larger one, as shown, right sides together. Trim the inner corner of each small square where it crosses the diagonal on the large square

3 Place 2 of the smaller squares on diagonally opposite corners of the large triangle with right sides facing and corners matching, as shown in Fig 9. Trim the inner corners of the small triangles in line with the crossing diagonal line on the large square so they aren't caught in the seam.

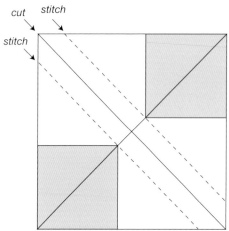

Fig 10. Stitch ¼in (0.75cm) either side of the marked diagonal then cut along the marked line

4 Sew ¼in (0.75cm) either side of the diagonal line marked on the small squares, as shown in Fig 10. Cut along the line between the rows of stitching.

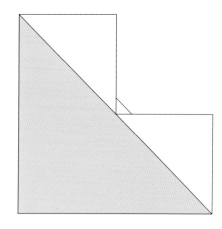

Fig 11. Press the seam

5 Fold back the smaller triangles on each piece and press in place. You now have 2 sections like the one shown in Fig 11.

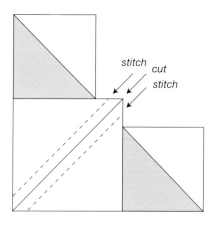

Fig 12. Position a small square as shown here and stitch ¼in (0.75cm) either side of the diagonal

6 Place 1 of the remaining small squares over the corner of each section with right sides together and edges matching, as shown in Fig 12. Stitch ¼in (0.75cm) either side of the marked diagonal line, as before. Cut along the marked line. Open out your units and press. You now have 4 Flying Geese units.

Making a diamond in a square unit

Fig 13. Diamond in a square unit

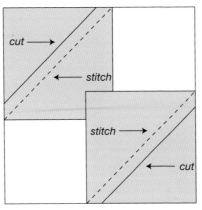

Fig 14. Place 2 small squares over the large square, as shown. Sew along the diagonal then trim

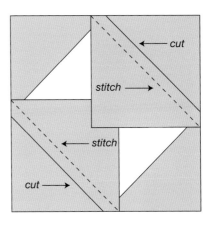

Fig 16. Attach the remaining squares as before

The square set 'on point' with triangle corners is another useful unit. Rather than cutting the corners as triangles, which make handling the bias edges difficult and, when working small, almost impossible to stitch accurately, these are cut as smaller squares, stitched then trimmed for a perfect result every time.

1 Cut the centre square the size of the finished square plus ½in (1.25cm). Cut 4 squares from the other fabric half the finished size of the unit plus ½in (1.25cm). Draw a diagonal line across the wrong side of each small square.

2 Place a small square in one corner of the large square and a second small square in the diagonally opposite corner with right sides facing and corners matching. Sew along each marked line. Now trim away the fabric ¼in (0.75mm) away from the stitch line towards the edge of the large square, as shown in Fig 14, above.

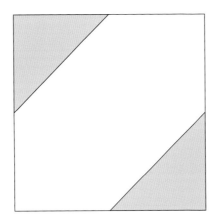

Fig 15. Press the fabrics over

3 Flip the triangles over and press as shown in Fig 15.

4 Repeat steps 2 and 3 on the remaining corners of the large square to complete the unit (Fig 16). Trim away the excess fabric beyond the stitching line, as before. Press the unit (Fig 17).

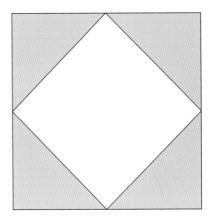

Fig 17. The completed unit

Putting the layers together

Once your quilt top is finished it needs to be matched with the wadding (batting) and backing and quilted together. If you plan to do your own quilting the 3 layers of the quilt must be made into a secure 'sandwich' first. If you plan to use the services of a long-arm quilter it is not necessary to layer the quilts as this is done on the machine. More wadding and backing is required around the edges of the quilt though – most long-arm quilters ask for an excess of 4in (10cm) all around each side so backing and wadding need to be 8in (20cm) bigger than the quilt top.

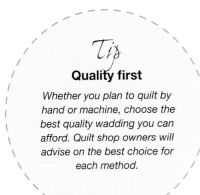

Tip

Quality first

Whether you plan to quilt by hand or machine, choose the best quality wadding you can afford. Quilt shop owners will advise on the best choice for each method.

Galaxy of Stars and Scraps was quilted on a long-arm quilting machine by Rosemary Archer of Frome Valley Quilting

Making the quilt sandwich

1 Check there are no loose threads on the front or back of your quilt top and press it thoroughly.

2 Prepare the backing by measuring the quilt across the centre both ways, then make up a piece of backing fabric which is 4–8in (10–20cm) bigger than the quilt top. Press any seams open to reduce bulk. You can use blocks and pieces of fabric to make a feature of the back or just use a single fabric. Wide bolts of fabric are available for backs in a limited range of patterns and colours, though you can always dye it to match your quilt top.

3 The wadding should be the same size as the backing. If it has been in a tight package it is a good idea to unpack it and drape it over a bannister rail or similar to allow it to breathe.

4 Lay the backing wrong side up, then the wadding on top and finally lay the quilt top right side up on top with an equal amount of backing and wadding extending all round the outer edges of the quilt top. This job is easier if you can find someone to help you with it.

5 Now secure the three layers together before quilting. You have three basic options here:

• Tack in a grid across the centre lengthways and widthways. Tack parallel lines of stitching about 4in (10cm) apart, starting at the centre. If you are planning to hand quilt this is the best method.

• For machine quilting you can use 1in (2.5cm) safety pins at frequent intervals across the quilt.

• Use a quilt tack gun or quilt basting sprays to speed up the layering process, following the manufacturer's instructions.

About long-arm quilting

The availability of long-arm quilting services is fairly recent in the UK. They have already been widely available in the U.S. Check the classified advertisements in your regional quilters' newsletter or the patchwork magazines for their details. Most of them will provide a brochure with their range of possible patterns and their prices. Operating a long-arm quilting machine requires skill and it is a good idea to see the standard of work available before

handing over your precious quilt top. If the process of quilting a large quilt seems rather a chore this is an option that is well worth considering.

Quilting the layers

I never mastered the technique of hand quilting, although I am a great admirer of the beautiful hand quilted work I see at the quilt shows, so my preferred method of quilting is by machine.

If you are a newcomer to machine quilting it is best to start with a smaller piece – a cot quilt or wall hanging. There are two ways to machine quilt; one is by using the regular stitches with the feed dogs engaged and the other is to drop the feed mechanism and free-motion quilt, which is a technique in which you have to create the quilting pattern by guiding the quilt through the machine with your hands. For preference I use the regular stitch, which I find easier to control.

Tips for quilting

• When your 3 layers are ready to quilt, begin in the centre of the quilt and work your way out to the edges. That way you will be less inclined to trap folds and bubbles when quilting.

• Try to devise a quilting pattern without too many stops and starts so there are not too many thread ends to dispose of. I tend to quilt without marking a design, allowing the patchwork pattern to dictate the quilting by outlining the patches and contour quilting around the block. Where there are larger spaces to be filled I use geometric patterns created with short lines such as zigzags, triangles and simple interlocking shapes.

• Consider the choice of thread. There are hundred of colours, including the variegated ones that change colour through the reels. I find these ideal for scrap quilts as the colours in the thread blend nicely with the colours in the patches, providing more texture and less of a hard line.

• If you can set your machine so that the needle stays in the work when you stop to turn, this makes quilting easier. Turning smaller pieces of work in the machine is not much of a problem but a full-size quilt can be quite a challenge.

• The free-motion method of quilting, in which the feed dogs in the machine are disengaged, gets round the problems inherent in turning large pieces of work in the machine as the quilt is moved backward, forwards and sideways with your hands as you stitch. Imagine making a drawing with the sewing machine needle as a pencil and the quilt as the paper. Rather than drawing by moving the pencil you are making the drawing – quilting pattern – by moving the paper i.e. the quilt. It takes skill to learn how to control the movement to create even stitches.

• Buy a good sewing machine – there is now a domestic sewing machine available which has a stitch regulator to make free-motion quilting easier.

• Wear quilting gloves for free-motion quilting to help relieve strain on the muscles when pushing the weight of the fabric under the machine.

• Practise with a smaller piece of work before embarking on a full-size quilt, and preferably work on a practice piece so that you don't risk a quilt that has taken many hours to produce.

Binding the quilt

Once the quilt layers have been stitched together you need to finish the edges and enclose the wadding. This is usually done with binding. Standard binding is cut from 2½in (6.25cm) wide strips and is easy to attach one side at a time. However, sometimes a wide binding will seem more appropriate and here it is better to mitre the corners for a neat finish. A broad binding will give an elegant frame to a quilt and is ideal if the block pattern goes right to the edge of the quilt with no border or if the quilt has a busy surface. Instructions are given overleaf for both types of binding.

I quilted Triangle Dynamics using a walking foot on the machine, which helps to prevent the layers moving at different speeds under the needle

Triangle Dynamics. Straight binding adds a neat, unobtrusive finish to this quilt

Adding straight binding with square corners

1 Trim the wadding and backing fabrics a scant ¼in (0.75cm) beyond the edge of the quilt top.

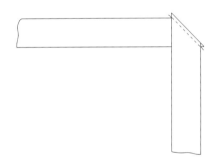

Fig 18. Join binding strips with a diagonal seam

2 Cut 4 binding strips 2½in (6.25cm) wide and of sufficient length for each edge of the quilt with a bit extra (see step 5). If you need to join strips to make up the length do this with a diagonal seam as shown in Fig 18 to reduce the bulk of the join.

3 Fold 2 of the binding strips in half lengthways, wrong sides together and press with a steam iron.

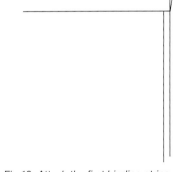

Fig 19. Attach the first binding strips to opposite sides of the quilt

4 Place the raw edges of the binding strips against the quilt top on opposite sides and pin in place. Stitch with the usual seam allowance of ¼in (0.75cm) as shown in Fig 19. Fold the binding over the edges of the quilt onto the back and hand stitch.

Fig 20. Stitch the ends of the third and fourth binding strips

5 To neaten the ends of the third and fourth strips of binding, cut these to the required length plus ¼in (0.75cm) extra on each end. Fold in half with right sides together

this time and stitch across each end, taking a ¼in (0.75cm) seam allowance (Fig 20). Turn each strip right sides out.

Fig 21. Turn the binding right side out and press it

6 Now press the strips along the length with wrong sides together and raw edges matching, as shown in Fig 21.

Fig 22. Attach the third and fourth binding strips

7 Position these binding strips on the remaining sides of the quilt, placing the neatened ends so they cover the raw edges at each end of the binding strips already attached to the quilt (Fig 22).

8 Machine stitch these strips to the edges of the quilt, taking a ¼in (0.75cm) seam allowance, as before.

9 Turn the binding strips to the back of the quilt and hem in place, paying particular attention to the corners.

Adding broad binding
with stitched mitres

The following measurements can be varied according to how wide you want the binding frame to be, and this will affect the amount of wadding and backing needed to project beyond the edges of the quilt top.

1 Trim the wadding and backing to extend to 1½in (4cm) beyond the quilt top.

2 Cut a binding strip 8in (20.25cm) wide and of sufficient length for each edge of the quilt plus some extra for the mitres. Piece these strips using a diagonal seam, if necessary (see Fig 18).

3 Fold the binding strips in half, wrong sides together and press. Place the raw edges of the binding against one side of the quilt top, leaving a generous tail of extra binding projecting beyond the edge of the quilt.

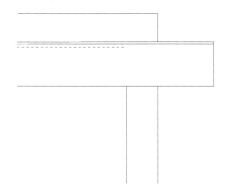

Fig 23. Stitch the first broad binding strip in place

4 Align the edges of the quilt top with the 2 raw edges of the binding and stitch to within ¼in (0.75cm) of the edge of the quilt top, taking the usual ¼in (0.75cm) seam allowance, as shown in Fig 23.

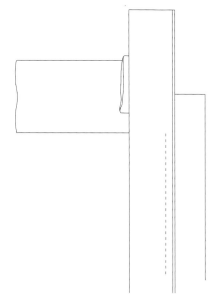

Fig 24. Stitch the second broad binding strip to the quilt

5 Press the binding away from the quilt top and pin the tail out of the way of the second binding strip to be attached. Position the second binding strip against the quilt top, leaving a tail for the mitre as before, and begin stitching ¼in (0.75cm) in from the edge of the quilt top at the exact spot where the stitching for the first binding ends. Continue to the end in the same way as before (Fig 24).

Four Patch Squares. Broad binding frames this quilt and is especially effective if there is no border on the quilt top

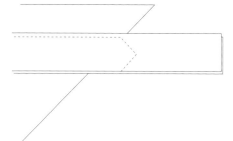

Fig 25. Mitre the corners of the broad binding

6 Once all edges have been stitched, fold the quilt diagonally at the corner so that the two adjacent bindings are placed together. Mark a dot on the folded edge of the binding opposite the point at which the stitching ends. Place the 45-degree line of the ruler against the edge of the binding and mark a line on the binding at this angle. Repeat from the point of stitching to the dot to make a V-shaped line, as shown in Fig 25. Stitch on this line with thread that matches the binding.

7 Trim the excess fabric away from the V shaped line of stitching and turn the binding through to reveal the mitre. Ease the point out with a knitting needle or similar tool and smooth the wadding and backing inside the binding at the corner. It may be necessary to trim a bit of the wadding and backing off the corner.

8 Repeat the process with the other corners of the quilt and then hand stitch the binding to the back of the quilt.

Acknowledgements

Thanks to:

George Hudson, my husband, without whose support and encouragement this and previous publications would not have been possible, love and many thanks.

Dianne Huck, Christine Porter, Judi Mendelssohn, Lynne Edwards and Barbara Chainey for advice, support, laughter and friendship.

June Morris for allowing me to raid her scrap fabric stash on more than one occasion.

Vivienne Wells, commissioning editor, for her help and confidence in me.

Rosemary Archer and Beryl Cadman for their long-arm quilting services (see resources below) and Fiona Law of 'The Cotton Reel', Worcester, for fabric supplies.

Jo Colwill of Cowslip Workshops, Launceston for providing a location for some of the photography in this book.

Resources

Quilting guilds
Joining a quilting guild is a good way to make contact with other quilters and discover what is happening in your area. Most quilting guilds have regional contacts and newsletters.

The Quilters Guild of the British Isles
Room 190
Dean Clough
Halifax HX3 5AX
Website: www.quiltersguild.org.uk

American Quilter's Society
PO box 3290
Paducah, KY42002-3290
Website: www.americanquilter.com

Quilters Guild of New South Wales, Australia
Level 5
276 Pitt St
Sydney
NSW
Website: www.quiltersguildnsw.com

Quilting magazines
A good way of identifying suppliers is to buy a copy of one of the quilting magazines. The advertisements in these will give you a comprehensive list of shops and services for quilters.

Patchwork and Quilting Magazine UK
Traplet Publications, Traplet House
Pendragon Close
Malvern
Worcestershire WR14 1GA

American Quilter's Newsletter Magazine
Primedia Inc.
200 Madison Avenue
8th Floor
New York NY 10016
Website: qnewsletter@pALMCOAST.COM

Australian Quilter Magazine
Express Publications
2 Stanley St
Silverwater
NSW 2128
Website: www.magstore.co.au

Long-arm quilters
If you don't want to do your own quilting, contact a long-arm quilter. You'll find addresses in quilting magazines. I have used the following experienced long-arm quilters for some of the pieces in this book.

Rosemary Archer, Frome Valley Quilting
335 Church Road.
Frampton Cotterell
Bristol BS36 2 AW
Email: Rosemary@frome-valley.co.uk

Beryl Cadman, Custom Quilting
Beal na Tra. Derrymihan West
Castletownbere. County Cork
Republic of Ireland
Email: patches@iol.ie

Quilting workshops
Taking a course helps you move on quickly. Ask at your local quilt shop:

Cowslip Workshops
Newhouse Farm, Launceston
Cornwall PL15 8JX
Email: info@cowslipworksops.co.uk
Website: www.cowslipworkshops.com

Index